Les McGehee
PLAYS WELL WITH OTHERS

Les McGehee

PLAYS WELL WITH OTHERS

Edited by
RIC WILLIAMS

Foreword by
OWEN EGERTON

Dalton Publishing

AUSTIN, TEXAS

Dalton Publishing
P.O. Box 242
Austin, Texas 78767
daltonpublishing.com

Printed in the United States of America
First edition, 2007

Edited by Ric Williams

Creative Design by Tamar Wallace, *tamargraphics.com*

ISBN-10: 0-9740703-2-7
ISBN-13: 978-0-9740703-2-2
LCCN: 2006935339

Illustrations by Aaron Mosier, *aaronmosier.com*

Cover Photography by Jason Flenniken

ATTENTION ORGANIZATIONS AND SCHOOLS:

Quantity discounts are available on bulk purchases of this book for educational purposes or fund raising. Special books or book excerpts can also be created to fit specific needs.

For information, contact Dalton Publishing, P.O. Box 242, Austin, TX, 78767, or email *deltina@daltonpublishing.com*.

To Christina, Marina, and Lucia.

Acknowledgments

I wish to thank the following people...

Owen Egerton, Steven Tomlinson, Sean Hill, Sharon Sutton, Saleem Assaf, Gary Kramer, Kimberly Chase, Tom Green, Jason Flenniken, Ben Bartley, Megan Bartley. Also Megan, Tyler, Jodi, Scotty, Petrie, Shoe, all my great improv friends, and ever lovin' Murdog. And the team at Dalton Publishing, especially Deltina Hay, Ric Williams, Amy Wink, and Tamar Wallace. And Lidia, Barbara, Bob and all the McGehees, Brischettos, and Palmieris. And Howard!

HOW TO USE THIS BOOK

This book contains three main sections. Section 1 features memoirs and road stories of an improvised life. Section B delves deeply into information about play and improvisation for life and business and includes research data. C-Section delivers the real deal handbook-style games and exercises that teach improvisation for novices and pros. And then there's the Enlarged Appendix with other tools to help you with your improvisation education. It's all described in the table of contents up front. Just like a regular book.

Some of you will want to focus on particular sections of this book and maybe skip around. That's OK. Each section has unique offerings so eventually you'll want to read them all. There are specific pointers for life, business, and entertainment. If you study this handbook you'll have a big head start on adding improvisation and some good play into your life and work.

Have fun!

TABLE OF CONTENTS

* *Games & Exercises*

PREFACE

Holy crap, I'm excited. I get to write this book! Me, a gangster mercenary of comedy. With an improvisation pistol in each of three holsters (one strapped over my heart), I am a show for the hiring. Made fresh daily. No preservatives. A hearty, heapin' helping of what you want. Hit the intro music...

Hi, my name is Leslie. I'm a guy. Yeah, I *know* you know a Leslie or a Lesley that's a girl. I'm a guy, with a great family, a home, good friends, and a personal career. I am a stalwart mercenary comedy professional working in Texas, across North America, and beyond. Fun Gun for hire. Improviser. You can call me Les.

While improvising, I have been fortunate enough to see a great many things around the world and I've seen what it does for the people who use it. I have seen improvisation turn people's lives around. I have seen improvisation launch marriages and families. I have seen improvisation bolster businesses. I've seen mean people get nice through improvisation. I've seen shy people get strong. I've seen bossy people become cooperative people. While improvising, I've seen tired people become energetic. I've seen exhausted people flow with ideas again. I've watched groups of people like each other again. While improvising, I have seen people's nervous tics go away. And during improvisation, almost everyone finds the type of laughs they've been missing, the great big overwhelming personal laugh.

I love performing and playing with improvisation, but passion, curiosity, and job opportunities have led me to study deeply as well, following where my ideas lead me and drawing from whatever diverse tools or concepts I find. I've developed and produced many training materials, articles, reports, professional organizations, conventions, and festivals in my pursuit of learning and knowing more about improvisation. And the more I learned, the more I wanted to learn, more and more forever. And this is still true for me.

I know that if more people accepted or practiced improvisation the world would be a better place. I have no doubt about that. Ask anyone who has practiced improvisation with a group and you'll see what I mean. It strikes right at the stuff that really creates the life experience. And it is fun! It releases you from the yoke of worry and miscommunication. It values trust and confidence, teamwork and communication, self and selflessness, and it is always beckoning you to do things the easier, better, and more fun way. And, oh my God, we want you to pause on your treadmill, lighten up, and join us for some fun.

You can have a better time. You can be smarter, stronger, and faster when improvising. You can have joy like you used to. You can like people again and look forward to their input. You can remember the sheer beauty of creation and remember how perfect things are. These things make you healthier and better looking! And did I mention that you can have fun and that you put your positive self into action more in your life?

Because I've played so many places and been hired by so many clients, I've known a great diversity of people. Because I get requested as a consultant, I've been able to work for and collaborate with an amazing number of experts from different industries. I've been privy to secrets, restricted areas, and glimpses of the future from all types of brilliant people who were tops in their industries and expertise.

My improv events are big fun. I have enjoyed about 5,000 of them. Up until approximately Show #2500, I remembered almost every one. It's natural since each event is unique and transformational. I often got to make stuff up with friends that I had trained, and was now able to employ. That usually feels like a party. We played together, managed festivals together, opened theaters and clubs together, toured together, traded training with the best professionals in improvisation from all across America.

This is my improvised career. I get to learn, perform, teach, train, write, and consult with improvisation. Improvisation is my vehicle. Improvisation has taken me to Hawaii, the

Bahamas, Mexico, Egypt, Greece, Italy, Spain, Germany, Holland, Belgium, Luxembourg. Also Los Angeles, New York, Chicago, San Francisco, up and down both U.S. coasts and in every major city across the Midwest. Also to Waco, Huntsville, Corsicana, Bandera, Buda, Elgin, Lubbock, Round Top, Dime Box (just Dime Box, not New Dime Box), and places that weren't even map-worthy. Big events and little events. I've been paid with big checks and little checks, but have always gone forward in my career. I've worked for club owners and corporate executives, from AT&T to the San Antonio Zoo. I've enjoyed quaint clients like church groups and monolithic clients like the U.S. government. I've worked on planes, helicopters, ships, boats, and in every type of environment. I've even worked incognito. I've had more good fortune and more weird-ass jobs than you could imagine. That is an understatement.

I meet people during heightened times in their lives. Their "special" days and nights, not only date nights but also Christmas, Passover, concerts, wars, bachelorette parties, vacations, kick-offs, award banquets, fund-raisers, family reunions, graduations, orientations, Mother's Day, New Year's eve, Valentine's day, festivals, and even funerals. Friday nights, Saturday nights, Sundays. I see people in high gear, adrenaline-filled people at the events that define their lives. At my gigs people have met, gotten engaged, gotten divorced, brought families in to see us. In my ComedySportz and National Comedy Theatre companies, a dozen players have met, fallen in love, and gotten married. Good strong matches and marriages.

My time in improv is a crucible of humanity. I feel like a vicarious psychologist. My path has been a museum tour of human choices. Between that and the constant training of workshoppers and performers I have seen sooo many human choices. This book is about what I've learned through my life as a professional, unfamous comedian, improviser, and entrepreneur. As a workhorse of the comedy industry, a pioneer of modern improvisation, a beacon to the business world, and a student of everything, I have found truths about life. Glorious truths that I must share.

I wrote this book because it is a good way to drive a dagger into the heart of the demon monkey on the back of so many people, the lying tyrant of worry, control, and unhealthy competition that makes so many people unhappy and limits their abilities to know success. Don't get me wrong, I believe in preparation, practice, planning; I believe in a lot of things, but success is elusive without balance and none of these things need our exclusive loyalty. Improvisation helps you value your assets evenly and allows you to use those assets to the right degree, at the right time, for the right reasons.

Reject Lying Monkeys

I see solutions to some of our personal and societal ills within the practices of play and improvisation. Play has ethics or it isn't play. There is open competition or it isn't play. Improvisation is how we carry these values with us in action. If there was more play and improvisation in the business world, for example, there would not only be more successes but also there would be better ethics. Improvisation and play prefer better ideas. No one minds if a capitalist gets rich on a great idea. It's those bad ideas with their bad business ethics and weak business structures that frustrate the consumer.

And we all need humor in our lives. I guess everyone doesn't need comedy, but everyone does need humor and play to stay in good form. I should say that again.

Everyone Doesn't Need Comedy, But Everyone Does Need Humor And Play

You deserve to have fun and thrive. Play and improvisation values contribution and moves quickly. It improves productivity while reducing miscommunication, stress, even missed workdays and insurance claims. It values the natural humor and beauty flowing around at any given time. And you can own it in your heart and soul and take it wherever you go.

Improvisation is done now, whenever and wherever that now might be. It can flourish in any moment. You can see it when you live in the moment.

When you are in the moment, you are at the crossroads of everything. You are at the crossroads of your education and your next thought, the intersection of your skills and beliefs, your past and your intentions; it is all accessible in that moment when you need it.

I think everyone can benefit from these reminders. I've proven this hundreds of ways in hundreds of diverse situations and have found it to be true consistently. Almost every participant of every show or workshop sees it, too. Life should be more fun and productive and I, and some of my fellow professionals, know ways to do that. I'm here to share it.

I know the monkey on your back lies to you. I'll tell you the truth about it.

— Yer Pal, Les

FOREWORD

I have seen Les McGehee conjure waves of laughter from crowds; I've seen him give more instruction to a young performer over a beer than they received from six weeks of pricey improv workshops; I've seen him work an audience of two thousand and an audience of two with the same passion and energy. In training events he's inspired nuns to dance, doctors to sing, and lawyers to almost smile. He has the rare talent of being able to find the funny in the room, pick it up, shine it till it glistens, and pass it around so everyone can have a touch. How did he learn all this? From me. I taught him all he knows. Except the unfunny stuff. That was someone else.

For over a decade now I've been performing with Les. We've done shows all across America, for stage, radio, television, and film. After each show, when the wild screams and nearly violent laughter have simmered down to a mild roar, I take Les backstage, pour him a cup of Earl Grey, sit him on my lap, and explain where he did well and where he needs to work a little harder.

"Owen, please," he says to me, his eyes shining like waxed pebbles in a sun-sprinkled mountain stream. "How do you make the people laugh so?"

And I tell him. And now he's telling you. You lucky noodles.

Oh, sure, Les had been doing comedy for years and years before we met, just not very good comedy. But he has come a long way, the little tyke. The only thing I've asked for in return for my years of wisdom and deep, comic compassion is the chance to write the foreword for this book. And a back rub.

Let me tell you a little about what makes a good improv comic. A good improv comic is splashing around in the cross streams of what is and all that might be. A good improv comic can make his mistakes work, he can take a decent idea and make it brilliant, and a brilliant idea and make it exquisite. A good improv comic takes the right kind of risks and creates a space where others can take the right kind of risks. He is always telling his fellow performers, "Go ahead and jump, I'll catch you." A good improv comic isn't just working to be funny, he's helping whoever is on stage with him to be funny, too. He knows that the biggest laughs are ones the scene earns, not just the individual. A good improv comic realizes that the tastiest ideas are those the group discovers, not the ones forced through by one person. He's not just shooting each time the ball comes his way, he's passing, he's blocking, he's making sure the team is playing as a team. Les is this kind of improv comic. The real good kind. I've taught him well.

And as the title of this book implies, Les plays well with others. He really does. That's more important than you imagine. How we play with others reflects how we live with others, work with others, settle conflict with others, and build with others. When everyone on stage is playing together, amazing things happen. Audiences laugh, but they also gasp in a kind of awe to see a group create something new and wonderful on the spot.

We see so many examples of lukewarm cooperation in our workplace, our government, and our families that we are starving to see individuals agree and create, whether it's in jazz music, comedy, or the dance-like improvisation of an excellent basketball team. God knows we need more of this kind of play in our world today. I'm not saying that Les' book is going to transform our society into a peace-driven culture of joy and laughter...but it might. Wouldn't that be cool?

So much can come from learning how to play well with others. And Les loves to play. He's made an art of it. Not just on stage, but in every part of his life. Les has carried the playful spirit of improvisation into his finances, his marriage, his style of parenting, his spiritual life, his cooking...just about everything. His businesses thrive; his marriage is a hot, sweltering, lusty adventure; his kids laugh, sing and make up games while the other kids on the block are zoning out in front of the TV; and his cooking...okay, his cooking isn't that great. But he does throw good parties. Les recognizes life as a series of *nows* to be celebrated. There are all kinds of wild and wonderful things happening right now! And the hard times, the problems? Well, when you've been making up things out of nothing for as long as Les has, you learn that no matter how dark the situation, you probably have everything you need to create solutions right at your fingertips.

Best of all for you, dear Reader, Les is playing in these pages. This book is packed full of stories, ideas, games, and a bunch of other stuff that's been floating around in Les' head for years. So sit back, you are about to have a very insightful and even inspiring conversation with one of the funniest comics alive today. Not the funniest. That would be me. But Les is probably in the top five.

— Owen Egerton

THE PATH OF AN
IMPROVISED LIFE

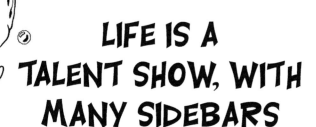

CHAPTER 1

LIFE IS A TALENT SHOW, WITH MANY SIDEBARS

You can discover more about a person in an hour of play than in a year of conversation. — Plato

When young Miss Butterfield met her first class of students she got so excited that she began arriving early every morning. She couldn't help it. She loved her students. She had the job she was meant to have.

Already she had planned a talent show. All the kids in grades 1-3 at Rose Garden Elementary would be in the show in one manner or another. She had gotten permission to use the little school's cafetorium and the music teacher was going to assist her. All the parents were invited and what better way to meet them than admiring their kid's talent?

She was off to a great start. She would "Never rest 'til our good is better and our better is best!" like the school motto encouraged. Each of her first four days of school was better than the previous. Until her first Friday. That's when the last student joined her class, Leslie David McGehee.

Leslie's Mom didn't have time to warn Miss Butterfield that he could be a bit precocious. He walked in with his Silver Surfer lunch pail wearing a green plaid blazer and a Beatle haircut, and the same listed items the other kids had been directed to have. He had his three-ring binders, his Big Chief pad, and the recommended pencils, crayons, Kleenex, ruler, compass, and other assorted stuff, which he quietly began stuffing into a desk.

Miss Butterfield had spoken to each child to find out about their personalities and families. She felt it especially important to celebrate each and every child and the talents they had. But Leslie had missed that discussion. She wanted to make little Leslie feel right at home so she started his first day with a "getting to know you" session. The entire class was rapt and quite focused on Leslie.

They had no idea.

Now, a Sidebar

Perhaps the funniest person in my family when I was growing up was my brother John. From the beginning, the best comedy experience I could imagine was being at our kitchen table over a card game late at night with the family. That still is a driver for me. But John was the funniest, most satirical, and irreverent of all my family.

My Mom was funny, too, or maybe it's more accurate to say that her Italian-ness gave me a joy and appreciation of life that has lifted me up all my days. She loves and laughs a lot. I dig life, like her. I know that's corny, but it's reinforced in my family from both the Italian and Irish sides of my heritage. I want to eat life, drink it, look at it adoringly, listen to it, roll in it, swim in it, make things with it, keepsake it, fight it, make love to it, and a little more of each of those all over again. Then nap. Repeat. On top of all that, my wife says I was surely a happy dog in a previous life.

You may have noticed I haven't mentioned my Dad. That's not because he was or is unimportant to me—quite the opposite. He passed away when I was two years, five months old. He is still a presence in my life in many ways. I feel fortunate about how my Dad is still in my life considering how little of him I got to share in the flesh.

Here's one for you. What's wrong with nearly every performer and why must we perform? That question has many answers, but one is that performers are trying to replace an irreplaceable loss. They want to get approval in such mass quantities that it eases the pain of what they are lacking from their childhoods. I'm not being tragic. I'm happy. I'm just sayin'...

Anyway, I'm talking about my brother John here. When I was five, I asked him about my Dad's passing and he told me a long story about it. I was on my front porch with two friends and a 45 record player. We were dancing to "These Boots Were Made For Walking" and "Kookie, Kookie (Lend Me Your Comb)" and generally having a great time. One of my friends asked me how my Dad died and I told him what I knew, that my Dad had been killed by a Bengali tiger whilst on safari in deep, dark Africa. I knew the details. He had tracked the animal for a great distance, through water, over mountains, and deserts, until he just had to take a rest. He leaned his tiger gun up against a tree to get a drink from a stream and he saw in the water's reflection the tiger sneaking up behind him. He turned and wrestled the tiger, trying to get to his gun all the while, but, alas, the Bengali tiger killed my Daddy in deep, dark Africa.

My Mom heard me telling part of this story and asked me how I knew it and I told her Johnny had told me. Further adding that he told me because she wouldn't have wanted to tell me the entire story. You might be getting the impression that John was a kid, but, no, he was about 18 at the time. It was years later that I realized what a ridiculous story it was. Mom almost sent him to join my Dad. Incidentally, my Dad had passed due to a coronary embolism. No tigers, no Africa.

Later, after I'd learned the truth, John told me, "Hey, you know what would be really funny? When someone asks how Dad died you could grab your heart like it really hurts, make a terrible face, and fall out of your chair saying, 'Call an ambulance!!' They'll think that's hilarious."

It's like a thing I heard Billy Crystal once say. When asked if he had been the class clown in school he answered, no, that he had been the class comedian. The class clown would, say, run across the football field naked during homecoming. It was the class comedian who had pulled him aside hours earlier and told him, "Hey, you know what would be really funny?" My brother John was, at this time, the family comedian. Years later he would forgetfully retell me the same long joke once in a while. It was a long joke about Roy Rogers and Dale Evans.

Seems Roy had bought some amazing shoes, but had stepped in mud upon arriving back at the ranch. He had put them on the porch for later cleaning. After dinner he and Dale went out and found that the shoes had been chewed up into little pieces. Roy was furious. He saw mountain lion tracks. He got his gun and told Dale he would kill that mountain lion if it was the last thing he did. He tracked the mountain lion (Bengali tiger) for days, over a great distance, through water, over mountains, and deserts, until he just had to take a rest. He leaned his (Bengali tiger) gun up against a tree to get a drink from a stream and he saw in the water's reflection the mountain lion (Bengali tiger) sneaking up behind him. He turned and wrestled the mountain lion, trying to get to his gun all the while...

At this point the story deviates from my Dad's passing story, for Roy succeeds in killing the mountain lion (Bengali tiger). I would stare at John in awe and disbelief at how he had informed me of this as parental history, but he didn't even remember and I liked the stories anyway. Just for the record...

When Roy gets back to Dale, minutes of story later, Dale sees him lugging that mountain lion and grabs a guitar, strums twice, and sings, "Pardon me, Roy, is that the cat who chewed your new shoes?" (Sung to the tune of "Chattanooga Choo-Choo," in case you didn't pick up on that.)

Now Back to Miss Butterfield and How I Got Into All This...

I was with Miss Butterfield in her classroom at Rose Garden Elementary. She explained that there would be a class talent show and I could choose a talent to display. I didn't know what to do.

Miss Butterfield sweetly asked me what my daddy did for a living. I was looking deeply into Miss Butterfield's lovely face when I said, "My Dad doesn't do anything. He's dead." She said, "Oh," attempting to recover, "Well, what did he do before he died?"

I locked sincere eyes with Miss Butterfield as she asked me the tragic question. I answered calmly, "Before he died he said...(I dramatically clutched at my heart and cried out)...CALL AN AMBULANCE!" And then I fell, wincing with mock pain, onto the cold tile of Rose Garden Elementary.

That poor lady was in asphyxiating shock. I knew in a flash that I had mistakenly taken that opportunity. The kids were all staring at me wide-eyed, frozen like I was Medusa. There's the problem with  SHE SAYS TO ME, 'LIFE IS FULL OF WHAT YOU WANT IT TO BE FULL OF. YOU OF ALL PEOPLE SHOULD PLAY WELL.'

a script, if it's inappropriate you're still stuck with it. Poor Miss. B. I looked at her and said, "I can juggle." Which was an immense exaggeration, but it got her off the hook. I learned a lesson in reading your audience.

My First Report Card

I figured I could probably juggle if I really wanted to, so I didn't rush into learning. Then things got worse when I came home with my six-week report card. It wasn't so good. I'd gotten mediocre marks for reading, writing, and arithmetic. And thanks to freaking my teacher out and slacking, I got a "Needs

Improvement" in the fourth item on the report card: "Plays Well With Others."

Mom asked me why I had gotten a "Needs Improvement" on Plays Well With Others. I told her I was bored, partially to justify my slackerism. She knew I loved fun, so she said, "That's stupid. There are great games and fun stuff everywhere." I was skeptical. She said, "If I can show you ten fun things right here and now, you'd probably have to admit that there're fun opportunities *always* and only a dumb person believes otherwise. Life is full of fun stuff everywhere just for you." She went further, trying to lock me into the deal. She said, "So, if I'm right, you would never be bored again, right?" Ten fun things and a customized infinite list seemed cool, so I agreed.

Mom whips out a pencil and paper and three great games go by, all fun. Then she is on the furniture playing hot lava with me. Out of the blue she becomes a monkey so I do, too. Then all the items on the coffee table formed a fantastic story community. Then we started playing a kick-in-the-ass tag game from her childhood in Italy called Boom Chia. Then we drew a picture together taking turns. We played a patty-cake game to Little Lambs Eat Ivy. We put on the soundtrack to Mary Poppins and she got me lip-synching and acting out our version of "Chim chiminey, Chim chiminey, Chim chim cher-ee." Then she taught me a game of push-button face gestures and we laughed until we hyperventilated. While she finished laughing, I laid my head on her tummy and let it bounce me with her belly laughs. I was slain. The only thing better than being funny was playing. God, playing is great. And you could just do it. And funny playing was twice as good. I was hooked.

She says to me, "Life is full of what you want it to be full of. You of all people should play well."

It sank in. I began to see it everywhere. If I engaged whomever, or engaged an activity, I had great fun and did better. It was amazing. Every book assignment, tetherball game, and conversation was a glowing thing full of promise. It was like the lights had been turned on and I could see the carnival all around me.

So, now I had a last few days to learn how to juggle. I felt like I'd made a deal and had to come through with a juggling show. At least I had that garish, green plaid sports coat that I could wear which I saw as half the battle. So I went home and asked my family if any of them could juggle. Nope. John did teach me how to *kinda* juggle two softballs though. I'd toss one in the air and move the other to the free hand, repeat, repeat. I was ready enough. Show day came and I was on the stage in the Rose Garden Elementary cafetorium and I had an odd but comfortably exhilarating feeling. I now refer to this as a Gaftop realization.

The Gaftop Realization

I had a great dog named Gaftop; he was a black lab. He was built for swimming, but he didn't know it. He had the usual webbed feet; slick, wide, flat tail, etc. One day I took him to the lake and tried to get him to swim and he was sure I was crazy. "Why would he do that?" he seemed to be thinking. Eventually I started playing fetch with him on the land until he loved the stick and the game and then I looked into his eyes and threw the stick a short distance into the water. He stopped cold and stared at it with his pulse racing. He shot me a look; I was still encouraging him with my eyes. He looked at the stick, at me, and then plunged in because I had implied it was OK and he knew I loved him. This is where the Gaftop realization occurred. He got the stick, but it was quickly overshadowed by his awareness that not only was he swimming, but he was made to swim! He looked at me with big eyes like, "Hey, look, Dad! I'm a swimmer dog!" And he was. The unimportant stick dropped from his mouth and he did circles around the lake. Got out. Jumped back in. Got out. Tried jumping from higher up areas. Swam more circles. It was one of his amazing days. Gaftop was swimming his joyous ass off.

Now back to the Rose Garden Elementary cafetorium. Talent show day. The place was packed. It was my turn, so I got my two softballs working. I felt the lights and the eyes on me and "Saber Dance" was playing loudly on the school phonograph. In the moment, I saw the entire room, its potentialities, the good lighting and the bad, the hot audience areas and the ones that needed to be made hot. And it flashed into my mind, "Hey, look, Mom! I'm a show boy!" I held the audience's attention for a couple of beats and then I went down into the house and worked it for the audience. I got on a chair briefly. When going from one row to another I did a dance step. My face was guiding the audience through the awe and surprise they should be feeling, then risk, then triumph, then adventure. Here, in a crouching position like I would pounce, then there, standing erect like a King. My story was masterful; in my victory over those two balls there rang an epic accomplishment. I worked the good areas; I brought the weaker areas to life. I went back onto the stage – HAHA! – it was a false ending – I had more! Back into the audience I went. The teachers and students and the whole house for that matter was in shock – laughing, gasping, and applauding shock. Miss Butterfield's mouth was hanging open. Again. None of us knew this was going to happen. When the music ended, I owned the cafetorium. I bowed like the Beatles at Shea Stadium. I held there patiently while the poor, slaughtered audience attempted to recover. Oh, the sweet taste of the kill. It was one of my amazing days. Les was showing his joyous ass off. I think I was channeling Red Skelton, Danny Kaye, Gene Kelly, Tim Conway, Sid Caesar, Imogene Coca, Lucille Ball, Dick Van Dyke, Donald O'Connor, Jonathan Winters, and who knows who else was there. At least that's how it seemed to me. I was king of the world. I thought, "This is it." If it all had to end here, then who could complain?

Really, I Have a Point Here

My point is this: it's night and day when you find out what you do. I believe this is true for everyone. But a lot of people superimpose what they want or have preconceived so thoroughly that it prevents them from taking their natural path. It's hard for these poor people. It takes so much energy to do what you don't naturally do! And when you find what you do, excellence, ease, and joy await. Always keep an eye out for the way something wants to go. It's the ride full of ease, fun, and cooperation. I bet that if this pertains to you personally, you know what your natural path might have been. And when you chose otherwise. And why.

And it's true what my Mom taught me about Playing Well With Others: life is full of what you want it to be full of. In improvisation we learn that there are gifts everywhere. Amazing ones. It's true abundance. And within it your path shines. That is, if you aren't too sure of something else ahead of time. I'd say that's presumptuous, to think you know before you really know. Like you'd go into Disneyland thinking, "Teacups! Teacups!" and walk right past Space Mountain and never see it. It turns out that Space Mountain is cooler. I hope your life isn't Teacups when it could be Space Mountain. Unless Teacups is what you love.

And Then There Was Gig

Flash forward to my senior year in high school and yet another talent show in a school cafetorium. But now I was the host. Hosting meant introducing the next act, introducing the judges, et cetera, but I took it to mean more. I wrote comedy material for it. I rehearsed. I planned to get some comedy in right after the sophomore magician and then again right before acrobat/dancer #3. For the first one I told a few jokes I had written. They were sooo bad I'm not sure anyone knew whether to have pity or concern. They all just stared at me like a cat that had burped. Comedy segment two came around and I sang a parody of "Yesterday," called "Leprosy!" I might have even borrowed the idea, if not the lyrics. Can't remember. Anyway, it worked and felt better. Note to self: musical comedy is easier than it looks.

"I CAN TELL YOU ONE THING, PAY A TEEN-AGER $125 FOR BEING FUNNY AND IT'S OVER."

The last comedy segment ended and there was the leotarded acrobat/dancer #3 waiting to dance to a nine-minute long Legs Diamond song (San Antonio rocks!). She was voluptuous beyond her years and the tension was palpable. Dads had renewed interest and Moms flirted with a momentary fight-or-flight response. But, alas, her record player wouldn't work. The old canvas-boxed institutional thing had ceased. Wouldn't revive. So she held her painful back bend waiting position while they tinkered, everybody feeling the pressure and showing professionalism way beyond the call of duty, way beyond proportion. Finally, the stage manager started making that taffy gesture at me. That universal pulling apart of the fabric of time between outstretched fingers denoting the need to "streeeeetch" whatever you are doing because the show can't go on yet. I had to fill some time.

I brought my buddy Howard up on stage with me for no reason. I think we did something funny. Then we danced. I have since learned that this is a defaulted position onstage: dancing without reason or context. Still time left. Someone asked me to tell a story they had heard me tell. I did. Someone asked me to tell a different story and I did. All comfortable. Time went by. The record player was now ready and we all got along to our soft-porn acrobat/dancer #3 lithely twisting and bending to Legs Diamond's "Searchin'."

Afterwards, one of the judges told me he didn't know the school had a comedian. I asked if he'd been watching how bad my jokes went. I thought I'd bombed because my jokes sucked. I certainly didn't think I was a stand-up.

He was more interested in the stuff I had done spontaneously, and the way I spoke with the audience. He said he had a benefit show he was producing the next night at the convention center and could use a kid to do stand-up as the opener. "It pays $125." Sold! I'm a stand-up. I can tell you one thing, pay a teenager $125 for being funny and it's over. Forget learning to plumb or engineer; he has found the money tree. Yeah, baby.

CHAPTER 2

COMEDY JOBS

*Work and play are words used to describe the same
thing under differing conditions.* — Mark Twain

I have had amazing comedy and improvisation jobs in my career. I've also had terrible jobs, odd jobs, and frightening jobs. My comedy jobs fuel my curiosity. I learned how to perform for multi-language audiences for Club Med. I learned about cell phone, Internet, and pharmaceutical technologies as they were emerging. I've learned immense amounts about everything from the window coverings industry to the hospital industry to the futurism industry. I learned from the best in television entertainment, computers, construction, consultancy, education, and dozens of other things. I've learned military life, politics, and global travel. I've spoken Spanish, Italian, and English on stage, as well as a dozen different gibberish dialects. I've toured nationally and internationally and always found people to hang with and enjoy the food, culture, and fun.

By loving the moment improvising, I have managed to find the most amazing employment I could never have imagined. It has been an amazing gift. Life has been much like my Mom said it would when I learned to Play Well With Others all those years ago. BUT I've also had stinker jobs. Oh my, I've had some stinkers.

The Good...
"HA"

This is it. It doesn't get any better than this. It could all stop here and why not? Who could complain? Look at my beautiful little daughters dancing in those grass skirts, shell necklaces, and flower leis. Their hair is highlighted and their skin is bronzed from days of swimming. Behind them there's a full Hawaiian band with drummers, conch blowers, and fire twirlers, and a Don Ho type crooning over it all while behind them is Anaehoomalu Bay and the beautiful Hawaiian sky before sunset. I'm distracted by the pretty wahinis walking back and forth along the buffet with flowers and trays of freshly cut fruits. Now here come the musclemen who have dug a roast pig out of a pit and are carrying it to the buffet on a huge tray. My beautiful wife Christina is sitting next to me, beaming, lost in the beauty, staring at our kids like I am, but taking it all in. My girls are getting an onstage hula lesson from a gorgeous wahini and I can see in their eyes that not only are they now experts but they are completely comfortable with being stars of the show.

> "I REMEMBER HOW LONG IT SEEMED THAT I STOOD CENTER STAGE, ARMS OUTSTRETCHED, FACE TURNED UP, FLOATING IN MY SEA OF GROUP EPIPHANY."

Suddenly my daughter Lucia, almost five, walks off the stage to whisper to me, "I'm a little tired, Daddy. You'll need to take over for a while." She thought she was carrying the show.

Like a flash I remember I'm working and I'm on. I climb onstage in character and explain to the sea of faces that we are looking for the last clue to identify the little returning princess to the island. They are into it. I reiterate the "clues" to the mystery we'd all discovered in previous outings and shows of that week. The foundation of this huge, multi-day event is perfect. If only I knew the big ending that I'm about to announce as the finale. I don't know the big ending yet and it's about to arrive. If I stay in the moment I'm sure I'll know when it's time. You heard me. I'm OK with the fact that I don't know what I'm about to announce.

I've told them, in a previous show and in a moment of excessive bravado, that, "We will know if we have found the princess when flowers rain from the heavens." You see, I know *some* secrets, like the helicopter loaded with flowers that is scheduled to clear the mountains and join us. But there was no helicopter practice! We don't know if weather will prevent it, how long it'll take to get there, if the flowers will blow into the ocean while the wind from the blades terrorizes the guests. Who knows? So I know some things, but how I'm going to put it all together, I couldn't say just yet. I've got to see who is there, choose a Princess that makes sense and who is the right distance from the stage, and cover the time until we're ready with the helicopter. Not a set of decisions I, or anyone else for that matter, has made before.

While I'm improvising some speech about the history of the Hawaiian Royals, I try to remember and orchestrate my cues, but it's hard to concentrate because no one has come up with the ending to our five-day game, including me, and I'm about to open my mouth and announce it – whatever it is. I'm not nervous, but I realize that I don't know what I'm going to do yet and I've got maybe a minute to vamp before it has to happen. At this moment I am Reginald Pithcairne, professional adventurer and historian, heart and soul.

There's my first cue, a pair of young Maori warriors run around the perimeter of the amphitheater lighting tiki torches with flaming clubs as the conch blowers begin emerging from the lush foliage around the perimeter. The conchs start up and the noise is part spirit and part music as their hollow howls merge loudly and oddly harmoniously. I still don't know what I'm going to do and I can't really think about it because I'm performing and orchestrating so many things when cue number two rushes into my mind: I see the helicopter cresting the mountain behind the amphitheater. I've got about 30 seconds to decide, act, get everyone into position without them knowing it, and execute my choice at the same time as cue three hits. I'm past ready to know what I'm going to do! I'm waiting for the solution to hit my mind like the flash I know so well. The drummers crank into high gear, the conchs are howling, hula dancers dancing; together they cover the sound and sight of the oversized chopper drawing near to overhead.

The time has arrived and I step forward and with a gesture... the crowd hushes. I wonder what I'm about to say; nobody's breathing. I'm standing in the middle of the moment when I get the flash. I gesture at a young girl in the middle of the audience and as if by magic the guys around her hear my need and pick her up in the air and trot her laughing, angelic form to the stage. I got the choice "right," verified by the crowd exploding with attention, laughter, and astonishment. And as she steps up to me onstage, I slowly put a big crown of flowers onto her head announcing as grandly and as joyously as I can, "We've found her! The Lost Princess!" As the crown touches her head, a half ton of orchid petals begin raining down onto the theatre from the big chopper. The crowd is having an out of body experience—laughing, crying, hugging, and throwing handfuls of succulent fresh orchid petals at each other.

I shoot a glance at Christina so she knows how good things are. I catch the producers' eyes and they are beside themselves. Like I said, I quit. The gigs don't get any better than this. I am King of Hawaii. I am momentarily King of the World. I am Elvis. My girls are rolling in orchids laughing. I remember how long it seemed that I stood center stage, arms outstretched, face turned up, floating in my sea of group epiphany. Just amazing.

The girl had been the perfect choice although I couldn't have known before then. She had won contests, been prominent in excursions, and generally was a great choice. Some of the audience had speculated on her already. Also turns out she was cute and wasn't too shy. You have to be an amazing judge of character at a glance to bring a stranger onstage in circumstances like that, especially a kid. Also she had to seem ready without asking and she had to be the right distance away and with parents nearby, etc. It all had to be right or I'd never have been able to work the timing.

Oh, and unbeknownst to me, she was the solution that the producers were wanting. Her father and his associates were so thrilled with how well it was handled that they asked us on the spot to create a similar event in Africa.

Well, that was an improv show. Yes, as in improvisation. Actually a 24/7, five-day long improv show. In Hawaii. With my family. I got a helicopter tour of the island on that gig, too. I even had a chance to visit other islands in Hawaii. Much nicer than the beaches where I worked in the Caribbean, nicer than the Pacific beaches I've visited at other gigs. Perfect!

The Bad...
"The Head Table"

I got the call from a great producer, one of the best locally and a friend, David Perkoff. He says he has this unique job he would like me to help with. It's a first try and he wants to know if it is a good thing for him to sell to his clients or not. The pay is good. It's a short job, but with an earlier call time than usual for makeup. It's at the nicest country club in town. If I like it, I can have two more that he'll book, each for good money. The gig is called "The Head Table."

It goes like this. There is a nice reception for business associates at an elegant country club. They mingle around an appetizer buffet for cocktails before dinner and talk about business and golf.

I've been made-up by a professional with Rambo-style jungle camouflage. A drab, greenish scarf covers my hair and my face has black and green all over it in leafy patterns. I'm dark enough that when I open my eyes widely and bare my teeth at the same time they brightly pop out and I look downright frightening. With my eyes and mouth closed, I am invisible, obviously. I say obviously, because I am unnoticed when inside the buffet. You heard me. My head is sticking up through the buffet table, shrouded in plants. I have been positioned under the buffet table since before the guests were let into the room. I have been watching the guests through almost-closed eyes. I have some tasty Brie, Kiwi, truffles, and chocolate-dipped banana slivers laid out in front of me like bait, elegant bait.

"I HAVE BEEN WATCHING THE GUESTS THROUGH ALMOST-CLOSED EYES. I HAVE SOME TASTY BRIE, KIWI, TRUFFLES, AND CHOCOLATE-DIPPED BANANA SLIVERS LAID OUT IN FRONT OF ME LIKE BAIT, ELEGANT BAIT."

I'm not comfortable. We didn't know how to judge the position and various discomforts ahead of time and now I know it sucks. And it sucks progressively more with each passing minute. My shoulders hurt up against the table. My legs have gone way past falling asleep or numbing. Those legs are now throbbing in the distance. I decide I've been stealthy long enough.

A guy in a suit walks up, chatting about the Houston Rockets and reaches for a snack. I let out a "PSSST!" briefly but pointedly. He pauses and glances around. I do it again. He looks in my direction but still sees me not. He stuffs an excessively large bite of fruit and cheese into his mouth as he leans over to peer more closely into my little thicket of bushes. All at once I push my face forward into the light while baring my teeth and widening my eyes and gnash out a lipless diction phrase, "How 'BOUT them ROCKETS!" and immediately pull my head back and close my eyes and mouth to become invisible again.

So the guy freaks. He shrieks like a little girl. Jerking his hands up in panic, he rains his scotch on all who stand behind him. He grabs his heart. His couple of friends around him who knew about me are hyperventilating, apoplectic laughing machines with the sound turned off. The guy can't catch his breath. He just stands there clutching his chest. He's pale. He doesn't know if he's OK. He might have shat.

Then out of the blue he says, "Let's get Pete over here and do that to him!" And so it goes for a while. It's a parade of innocents and veterans. I try whispering to some and then disappearing without returning. I tried popping out to advise against the salmon and disappearing. I did a lot of winking in the dark. This goes on for 20-30 minutes.

Then a big, smiley, bouncy, robust man trots up and grabs a snack and I pop out and say, "Save a little for me, will ya?" And his reaction is to jump straight up. No kidding, the guy is 300 pounds, going horizontal towards me in some super-human fight-and-flight simultaneity. On his way up he's grabbing a handful of fruit and cheese and tossing it at me like tossing sand in the face of a bear to let it know you aren't going to die quietly. His mouth is agape and his tongue is folded up and backwards. His eyes are pinpoints of pupils on veined ping-pong balls. I'm thinking I've killed a man and am about to be crushed under his falling, dead body sporting elegant buffet and wearing Rambo makeup, in a bizarre comedy-related accident that will never be explained.

I live. He lives. The client loves me and hates me. They had the best of times and the worst of times. They got out of there looking over their shoulders like the table was still dangerous. Elegant, but dangerous.

I tell David the producer that it sucked but could be made to work. I do another one like a glutton for punishment. This time the crowd is passing by, not hanging out too long. Also the buffet table is twice as big and elaborate, with two holes for me, one at either end. I have a nice little padded rolling seat just the right size. This time we try a Caribbean theme and I wear pirate make-up complete with a display parrot on my shoulder.

The clients this time are a big bunch of lawyers touring a restored historic building. I get to pop out and say things like, "Hello, liar!" This I claimed was how a pirate would pronounce "lawyer." Gig was better controlled and the client loved it. I booked two more Head Table gigs and gave them both to my pal Joe and let him know the tricks. Now I take "above the table" gigs exclusively. I think.

...and The Ugly
"The Gig-That-Cannot-Be-Named"

It's after Thanksgiving and the last panicked holiday party bookers are calling. This client calls from a local television station and says she wants us to entertain at their party. She hasn't seen our show though, so we invite her to the theater. She is concerned that we will do material that is inappropriate. She wants to know what we'll be making up, which, of course, can't be answered, but some people ask for it. She is more than a little persnickety and they don't have money and want a deal from us. I should have seen the warning signs by then, but no.

So the client comes to visit the theater with some guests. One of the things we perform is a parody of a local news show. This particular improvised sketch played off of a dashing anchor, grinning sports guy, panicky weatherman, and various reporters and such. Client loves it. Demands that we do it in her show.

Show is at an old Masonic temple that has a beautiful, old theater with great woodwork and details. There is a problem for the client though. The local university is playing for the division championship and the game is on in the historic parlor. Many of the guests don't want to leave the TV. The client has bought a show for them, has a multi-course dinner about to be served, and has brought a truckload of merchandise to give away such as DVD players, stereos, I-pods, even some TVs. You heard me. They are going to give it away if they can get the guests to leave the TV. It's not enough. The guests don't want to budge. We are delayed and hanging out in this incredible and spooky Masonic temple.

Client comes to me and says she wants to delay again and I say, "OK." I'm bored and hungry and in a cool old building, so I go exploring and find the kitchen. I've got my buddy and fellow performer Scott with me. We walk down into the basement kitchen and chat some snacks out of the chef. Then we notice more, narrower stairs going down across the room. We take these and we're in a conference room a floor and a half below the theater. Across this room I see narrow stairs going up, they switch back and continue up. Then a curtain opens onto a large oval meeting room done up floor to ceiling in green felt. There are no corners; they've been rounded. There is an ornate table with a dozen or so carved wooden chairs around it. There are a few gold scepters on carved wooden shafts several feet high and on stands. There are a couple of gold trays with things written on them in another language. MUY CREEPIOSO!

We get out of there and eventually the client decides to start anyway, even though many won't leave the TV in the parlor. They don't want dinner or free merchandise, and they certainly don't want comedy. Meanwhile, all through these delays, the skeleton party crew of TV personalities and their spouses and girlfriends has passed the time drinking and chatting and drinking some more. They are now a little more than toasty tipsy and way past ready for dinner.

As we head back to the stage I catch a glimpse of our client crying and pleading to the blank-faced fans in front of the TV. She's got a DVD player in a fancy box in her hands and she's crying, "Why won't you come in? We planned all of this for you! We have DVD players and TVs. Come on! What do you want from me? WHAT DO YOU WANT FROM ME!?!?"

The DJ plays our introduction music. We go on. The sound and lighting are marginal. We have mics on stands so can't really move around much. The audience is sparse and patchy, distant, disoriented, and drunk—out there somewhere in the dark.

We do OK, briefly. Then we do some stuff they find offensive, or they couldn't hear us, or they were all simultaneously nauseous or something. Scott tosses off a reference to the Columbine High School massacre. I can't believe it. I try to save it with an after-comment. I fail miserably and make it worse. There's no damn comedy in those dead teens. Now they hate us. We still have the sure-fire sketch though. So we launch into the news sketch. Turns out we hit all the sensitive elements of the news crew. They felt personally attacked and mocked. I'd even say they were flabbergasted. I've wanted to use that word for a long while, but I only use it here because it is accurate. This wisp of an audience was now overwhelmingly flabbergasted. We decided to change gears and try to get something funny out before we had to leave the stage and we jump into building a quick comedy scene using audience suggestions. Bad idea. Some of the TV personalities had gotten drunk enough to yell offensive stuff to us, guffawing at their own cleverness. The client stood up and started the repeating mime action of cutting her own throat, or ours I guess, in the universal sign for stop it.

We ignore her. We wanted one more try to redeem our show. We'd had sooo many successes we couldn't fathom bombing so thoroughly. A weekend anchor yelled something *almost* too unintelligible to be offensive. He yelled something like, "Clinton and Monica!" His pregnant wife shrieks loudly over his laughs, "YOU KNOW ENOUGH ABOUT AFFAIRS ALREADY!" By then the client was standing five feet in front of us slicing her throat like a wide-eyed, OCD Marcel Marceau.

"YOU HAVE TO HAVE A RELATIONSHIP TO FAILURE TO CONTINUE WITH JOY."

We did something I'd never done before. Or since. We sprinted out the side door. We went straight to a bar and tried not to think about it. But it hung in every silence. We had show death on us like skunk. It was no use. It stays with you forever in some ways. You have to have a relationship to failure to continue with joy. And that's what we did. But it was a quiet, still night the rest of the evening. We patiently waited for the next show. It couldn't come quickly enough.

CHAPTER 3

BUSINESS FINDS ME

It is not the strongest of the species that survive, nor the most intelligent, but the one most responsive to change. — Author unknown, commonly misattributed to Charles Darwin

Thankfully, I don't have so many wild stories about business training.

I didn't get this deep into improvisation training on purpose. I was requested, and I responded, and found it productive and fun and good. But business has always found me, not the opposite. I get a call, or someone saw a show, or recommendations get made.

I love teaching improvisation to diverse groups. I love spreading the word in all ways. I know they need it; everybody does. I also know I do a good job. I like to do a good job. I like the excellence we achieve in training, too. Results from my training are not only effective, but they are tried and true, proven and measured. And I have no problem laughing and having fun myself while working.

For the first 10 years or so, companies would simply find me. They were all looking for solutions and advantages and a bunch of them came up with similar conclusions and sought me out. I am constantly amazed and flattered by this part. It was a natural fit and I loved it. I still do. A lot of improvisers can't teach well. If they can teach well, they might not love it. I never had those burdens. I am the double-speed Mr. Rogers of Improvisation, happy to go to work. I am the Johnny Appleseed of Improvisation, planting seeds constantly and grinning all the way.

I got hired locally, and then beyond. Word got around a little more and I started getting referrals. Bit by bit, I got hired by most of the best and largest companies. But it started out slowly and systematically. Here's the story of how companies and groups began finding me.

The Great State of Texas

So I'm doing a ComedySportz show on Sixth Street in Austin. It's kinda like Bourbon Street. We had opened a club there by the famous Esther's Pool called, "The Deep End at Esther's Pool." We were doing a show on a Saturday night and afterwards a lady comes up to me and asks how we get to be so quick and creative. I say that we train and practice. She asks me if I could teach the same stuff to employees of a state agency. She was there with her boss and he was curious. I say that, yes, in theory, I could, but not much of that had been done.

The truth is that I knew how to teach a bit, but I didn't really know if it could be done with "civilians." I figured that I could figure it out if I needed to. Honestly, at that point I was thinking two things: that they were full of crap and that they drank *all* the scotch.

The lady continues to tell me that her boss is the State Comptroller of Public Accounts at the Texas State Capitol and might want me to train his entire staff. *Sure*, he would (I thought). I suggested that they contact me Monday morning. She said they would. *Sure*, they would (I thought; I'm so smart). Goodnight, Ms. Scotchy McScotch. Done and done.

So, I get woken up by the phone on Monday morning by a call from the State Comptroller's office asking me if I can come in for a meeting. They say I should plan on telling them how the workshop will go. Well, I didn't know how it would go, but I did schedule the meeting.

I asked them how many people were in the group, how much time I was going to have, and what goals they were trying to achieve. They wanted better communication and teamwork, some stress reduction, and, hopefully, some fun. I would have 65 participants in each group, two groups, two-hour sessions.

What the heck? I took a shot and wrote an outline of exercises that seemed pretty good. I was a little concerned with how to manage that many participants, so I called ComedySportz training guru Bob Orvis in Milwaukee who had done a few of these things and he gave me some ideas. Then I lined up a couple of my best players to help me, and, presto! We had a plan for a workshop.

Like many other industries, the best improvisers in America all kind of know of each other. This has always been true. Especially back then when there were so few professionals. To this day, I often hire my best counterparts when the job calls for it. So I knew that there were only a couple of other guys who might know how to do this level of work and Bob was one of the best options for advice.

Anyway, I had this little bit of a plan and I went to the meeting. I was hired. How much would it cost? I thought they probably had plenty of money. I mean, after all, Texas is the 11th largest economy in the world or something, right? So I hit them hard.

"$250."

"$250?" they asked. I freaked on the inside. I just knew I had asked for too much. But they agreed immediately, all nodding to each other around the table. Then one of them asked, smirking almost imperceptibly, "For one workshop or for both?" "Total," I said. I didn't understand at the time what the cat-eating-the-canary grin on their faces was all about. They generously booked me at $330 for the two workshops. Woo. Hoo.

At the event Mr. Sharp, the Comptroller, passed by and said he'd heard how good we were doing. He said that the services we were offering were worth MUCH more than $250. I told him thanks for telling me. They got me to do one another year and I doubled the price. It was still a fraction of what I should have been charging to be in the ballpark of what they usually paid for professional training.

So I learned the first of many pricing and value lessons. But I also learned that I could indeed teach any group of people, not just comedians and actors. I could teach them quite well even. We got rave reviews and many new comedy customers out of the deal. Plus, many of the participants requested us for their new companies when they eventually moved on. I liked that I could teach these civilians to improvise. I liked that they laughed their butts off and seemed like nicer people leaving than they did coming in. I liked getting the word out. I think this was in 1989.

UN Desk

It was for the Comptroller that I first used a design purely of my own imagination. A key part of it was an exercise I'd created called **UN Desk** that exercised communication levels through the use of matching gibberish languages. It is very fun and dependable and one of the finest things I have built.

UN Desk was so successful that a couple of participants spoke languages we didn't know and passed them off as gibberish. Swahili was one and that person's exercise partner roughly spoke it as well just by using the listening and matching techniques taught in that communication exercise. *UN Desk* is hilarious and is so unbelievable. It's like seeing a cat talk. Of course, the participants get to share in the surprise.

The scene for *UN Desk* is simple enough: a desk outside the Great Hall at the UN. All the workshop participants are delegates. We all speak each other's languages. We respond in whatever language we are approached with. Two chairs are handy for this exercise. They both face forward but slightly inward and a few feet apart. The chair on the left is Player One and they are the catcher. Player Two chooses a fun style of gibberish language and enters to converse briefly with Player One. Player One listens, responds; there is give and take. Players can practice listening and communication skills and agreement and empowerment and reuse pieces of language that get introduced into the conversation. The results are amazingly communicative. We all know what they are talking about if they stay intent on each other. I'm not sure it communicates into print but it is an amazing little machine of an exercise.

The Hicks

A nice lady came up to me at the end of a show and asked if she could rent out the theater and have us do a private show for her husband's birthday party. This lady would help to change my life. Her name is Priscilla Hicks.

Shortly thereafter, the Hicks' company had a big event planned on a dude ranch. Ray Hicks, Percilla's husband, admired the Adventurer's Club at Paradise Island in Disneyworld. I agreed that they did the best job at that sort of thing. Ray had seen Disney embed performers in an incentive travel group in Acapulco and thought it was a lot of fun, but could have been done better. We kind of recognized each other as mischievous kin. We decided to give it a go.

Well, it turned out that Priscilla and her staff were really good at building events. I learned a lot by brainstorming with them. No matter how wild some of the ideas were, we found lots of success. We took leaps of faith in our design plans for these large groups of clients.

I attended the dude ranch gig as Bud Gitcher of Gitcher Blinds Window coverings operating out of Mexia, Texas—*real* hicks. "Bud" was famously successful in the window coverings industry, whether anyone knew it or not. My wife Punkin and I arrived at the rendezvous point riding in the back end of a pick-up with our clothes in plastic and paper bags. It was an extreme acting job, complete with costuming, physicality, altered voices, and studied effect.

I had learned enough about window coverings to bluff expertise. I'd put so much weirdness into that expertise that it was unbelievable. But, when some guests strongly suspected that I was full of crap, I'd lay out some more appropriate expertise and they'd decide I was legit after all, just a freak. Bud had also become independently wealthy from a separate entrepreneurial idea that Punkin and he had developed: the combination Trailer Park/Drive-in Movie Theater. What a blast!

I entertained and mystified to secretly keep events moving. Then we'd clean ourselves up and teach a professional business improv workshop. These were so loved that people didn't recognize us as Bud and Punkin. It was amazing and we were blown away at how much fun and successful the whole thing was.

Meanwhile, the Hicks' had purchased the services of a great comedy group for a big night at the event. Priscilla's Mom and Dad, Gus and Pearl, were hosting the event dressed up like a gingham cowgirl and her Frito Bandito beau. They were a hoot, true originals.

My associate and I did improv comedy to open the show, and then the big touring show came on. The touring show wasn't received very well and was cut short. It was inappropriate for some families and even some adults. So we went back on and did a little more improv comedy and it all went over great. Then we all danced and drank.

I was in my element. The Hicks' may have been clients, but they were to become more. They are fun, skilled, and good people. They are like family to me. I ate a little extra barbecue and had another beer while I watched Gus and Pearl bounce about the dance floor. A fine night.

That next morning we were up at dawn to get the day's events going. Before we could get out of our rooms there was a knock at the door and we were informed that Pearl had passed away during the night and the family had all gone into the city to

'I LIKED THAT I COULD TEACH THESE CIVILIANS TO IMPROVISE. I LIKED THAT THEY LAUGHED THEIR BUTTS OFF AND SEEMED LIKE NICER PEOPLE LEAVING THAN THEY DID COMING IN.'

take care of things. I was put in charge of running the morning meeting and daily events with a couple of members of the Hicks' staff. We stepped up and managed to have fun, not in spite of, but more in honor of Pearl and her fun-loving way at these events. It was both tragic and great to be a part of it all.

I continued to develop these fake-expert travel events with the Hicks' and I ended up doing many of them, almost all in exotic locations for days at a time. I used acting skills combined with design and comedy. I even wrote up the theories about this type of entertainment, based on some theatrical principles espoused by Bertolt Brecht. It was by doing my best to answer the creative challenges the Hicks' offered me that opened those avenues.

I performed for the Hicks' on ships, planes, and helicopters. It was the Hicks' who took me to Hawaii the first time, the Bahamas, too. To this day, their family company did some of the best events I've ever been part of.

AT&T

I did a cool event for Cellular One, which became McCaw Communications before it became AT&T Wireless. They had change management issues with these transitions and I helped them through it.

I had just missed out on a job by bidding way too low on it. I was determined to quote higher for the next gig. So, when the client asked what I thought my bid would be, I gulped and forced myself to say twice as much as I first had in mind. I could tell from her reaction that it was an acceptable price and by no means too high. And then I kicked ass for them and got rehired a bunch of times.

The big boss came through and was freaked-out happy. He thought it was just a great event and such a bargain. He told me I was more valuable than Tony Robbins. I didn't know who Tony Robbins was, but I could tell he was comparing me to the best in his mind.

I have learned price lessons over and over again. The biggest recurring mistake I made was undercharging. The second most frequent mistake I made was in not figuring out budgeting categories and in not understanding companies' purchasing

'HE TOLD ME I WAS MORE VALUABLE THAN TONY ROBBINS. I DIDN'T KNOW WHO TONY ROBBINS WAS, BUT I COULD TELL HE WAS COMPARING ME TO THE BEST IN HIS MIND.'

practices. As I developed my skills I caught up, but I still don't try to maximize my take on an event. I do, however, know what the pay ballpark is for various events and I work within that to make it easier on all involved. That information is hard to come by and is a benefit of high mileage and building great relationships.

MBA Schools

In the last five years I have done a lot of work with graduate schools of business. They found me by looking for innovative solutions and advantages for their MBA candidates. My training fits into that environment really well. I think they are excellent clients for a couple of reasons.

They have an understanding of what they are developing and sustaining and they have the ability to support the work. They are highly educated and they get it. And for those same reasons I find them to be excellent for getting the message out. They are hungry for the message and as business leaders they will have far-reaching impact that will carry the message further.

One of the brilliant people I get to work with is a guy in Austin named Steven Tomlinson. I met him years ago as he ventured into performance through storytelling. We worked the same theater, the now-defunct Chicago House in Austin, and made it one of the prime places to hone our craft. In Chicago House-style, we shared the bill with musical greats like Charlie and Will Sexton, Jimmy LaFave, Ronnie Spector, and Jo Carol Pierce, as well as dance troupes, theatrical productions, comedy sketch companies, poets, you name it.

I came to find out that Steven is a highly respected economist, MBA educator, and administrator. He also teaches at seminary and is an award-winning playwright. He has greatly influenced my message on productivity, ethics, and true success.

He was leading an advantage program at the University of Texas McCombs School of Business called Plus. He had taken some improv classes and decided that the MBA candidates needed our training. He commissioned me to partner with a competitor and write a full curriculum for 400 MBA candidates: a comprehensive improvisation curriculum with over 70 structures, a handbook, and a teacher's guide.

It was a brilliant move for all involved. I partnered with Sean Hill of the International Theatresports board. Theatresports was one of the most developed improv performance and training outfits other than ComedySportz. The two formats have basic differences in philosophy. Putting us together was great for my development. We wrote a fine program and hired the best teachers coast to coast. Sean and I had fun and even launched a company together.

They gave us all 400 students for a week for several years in a row. The curriculum worked great first try and improved each year. I still see some of those participants and they always thank me profusely. Some of them have since hired me themselves. They wear me like a feather in their cap.

Steven introduced me to other great educators at UT, Saleem Assaf and Leslie Jarmon. With them I continue to find innovative ways to get the message of improvisation and play to UT grad students. With Leslie we have even developed social interaction models with improvisation that are quite groundbreaking. These fine people are examples of how great educational minds find each other and I am humbled and fortunate to hang with them. When you get the chance to work in a circle of people like this you can only come out of it smarter. Nice work if you can get it.

Steven, meanwhile, moved on to guide and teach for the new Acton Entrepreneurial MBA program. It is a small, innovative, and intense program, that is already one of the most respected in the nation. It's a great program that will have a lot of highly active entrepreneurs coming out of it, so I'm happy to be able to get my message out through Acton.

The MBA curriculum I now use is called Improvisation for Business. The areas of this curriculum can be done together or separately. The core elements included in the curriculum are creativity training, collaborative skills, communication skills, networking skills, meeting skills, brainstorming skills, credibility skills, presentation skills, leadership skills, listening skills, stress management skills, teambuilding skills, status issues, confidence and risk, and change management. I couldn't have built the Improvisation for Business program without experiencing Improv MBA.

Networking

MBA grads lead me to companies and companies lead me to MBA schools. They often share the same training needs. They certainly share the same talent pool. They allow themselves to give top education and training as a cultural value, often to people they can't even hire.

Case in point: a UT alum introduced me to the Pepsico/FritoLay/QTG people who have hired me for years now to do an annual event for the Consortium for Graduate Study in Management, which is a national group of the best MBA schools. In general, top MBA candidates from across the nation are vying for internships and job positions with the companies that host and support the consortium.

I created a networking program for these MBAs that includes a live presentation and a video. It is built from the best networking and related info from my Improvisation for Business curriculum, but customized for this company and the consortium. Most of the MBA candidates who attend the consortium events are not hired by the sponsors, but they all leave having had the best training for networking skills available.

A company in an endeavor like this creates a culture of ambition, support, humor, and excellence that gives them a very strong image. The networking skills we teach have great ancillary effects, too, like communication skills, stress relief, and others. Everyone has a better event. Everyone benefits.

Clients Who Care

A while back, I chose a player from an audition in San Antonio. Her name is Sharon Sutton. She is an education specialist for the U.S. government, though I didn't know it at the time. Once she got the message of improv and play and how it worked, she couldn't wait to turn her education associates on to it. She and her associates organize training for a huge number of professionals with the Veterans (VA) hospitals. She's a top trainer herself.

For years I have trained for various groups from the VA. They are a unique group of people and I am proud to help them. The VA is unequivocally determined to do the best they can for their clients, many of whom have no other options outside the VA.

Annually, I train at their Leadership Development Institute. They have a core of education administrators and trainers who I have learned from while teaching with and for them. It is important to have clients who want to do the right thing and support their members. Especially because of my time entertaining the troops overseas and having a veteran brother, I am keenly aware of the good works they do at the VA.

I'd have to say the same about Seton Hospitals, Santa Rosa, and several of the other hospitals I've helped. These non-profit hospitals are full of amazing people doing amazing things. I love helping them. Plus, the nuns giggle when they drink wine.

Communication, Collaboration, Creativity, Teamwork

These are some of the main topics I get hired for. All of them fall under the larger heading of Improvisation for Business Skills and also Team Development. Almost every curriculum I use has a communication core, since lack of communication is what exacerbates so many business problems. Leadership rings clearly through improvisation and can be taught simultaneously with some of these other topics. Teamwork is prevalent throughout the message. They are all fun.

Change Management

Our only security is our ability to change. — John Lilly

Change management is an amazing improvisation topic. The improvised life is built for change management. It is a type of engagement that lessens the incidence of failure and employee attrition. Actually, it ignores the paradigms of failure and attrition. It also creates a natural sense of communication, follow-through, and fulfillment. It is the stuff that the fabric between us is made of.

Improvisation helps with change management by keeping things moving in the right direction with increased engagement and reduced attrition. It enables teams to follow their planned change with  increased productivity and reduced stress. It approaches change management similarly to how the human condition approaches group problem solving. We keep each other in synch and in process. We are built to do well with change given the right support, and improvisation is a great enabler of that.

Change is easiest when the entire team is engaged, and improvisational principles reinforce that. When we keep each other "in," we maintain better progress than individuals can accomplish on their own. That goes further to improve our confidence.

King Whitney Jr. said this about change...

> *To the fearful it is threatening because it means that things may get worse. To the hopeful it is encouraging because things may get better. To the confident it is inspiring because the challenge exists to make things better. Obviously, then, one's character and frame of mind determine how readily he brings about change and how he reacts to change that is imposed on him.* (Wall Street Journal, 6/7/67)

And it is fun. Talk about making lemonade out of lemons. Improvisation engages everyone and enables the change process. Improvisation training during change can bring you through as a stronger company. Change management is easier over time when the staff has the necessary values in place.

Motivation, Stress Reduction, New Staff, Kick-offs

These are other common reasons to hire me for comedy or training improvisation. These are usually ancillary benefits derived from my improv work. For instance, motivation is not a goal I choose to emphasize, but it is true that my training creates lots of motivation. Same with stress relief; it is a natural side effect. But I have developed outlines to drive straight at these topics when asked to do so.

I get challenged on new topics regularly. And thank goodness business finds me.

CHAPTER 4

"WHAT DO YOU DO?"

Creativity makes a leap, then looks to see
where it is. — Mason Cooley

Suffice it to say, I can barely describe what I do for a living. It makes family reunions a pain. Most of my jobs don't even resemble each other. Many have been great, but many have been purely bizarre.

If I say I am an improviser, the ones who know what I'm talking about think of either *Whose Line Is It Anyway?* or some odd amateur group they've seen or a class they've taken. If I say "comedian," they ask for a joke or worse, tell me one. I don't know any jokes usually. That confuses the heck out of people. They give me the, "Oh, crap, you'll go broke" look when I've said I'm a comedian yet I don't know any jokes. Then in the middle of dinner or something there's a big laugh and some-one will say, "Les'll use THAT one in his routine!" As if I have a routine. As if I'll remember that joke.

When I first started performing improvisational comedy shows and told folks about it at the end of a show or some-thing, Texans would raise their BS detecting eyebrows and say, "You just stand there and make stuff up?" I'd explain that we are making it up, but, like jazz, we have skills and a structure we use for a show. This explanation was usually met with silence, confusion, and general frustration. I'd continue that, "Yes, we make stuff up, but we do sketches like you might see on Saturday Night Live." Honestly, that never worked much either. Thank goodness the work was funny and some people found us and then found us again.

Many a family gathering has had side conversations about what I do for a living. "He has a mortgage and a family; where does he get his money?" "I hope he isn't doing anything illegal." "He's like Robin Williams." Or worse, they would call me over to say, "I'm trying to explain to Uncle Albert what you do for a living…"

I used to answer more plainly. I'd say, "I'm a 'comic.'" Or a "trainer." Later in life I'd sometimes say "consultant." I've gotten quite accustomed to blank stares. I don't blame them. I bear the burden of the unexplainable job.

I write and produce, often with rehearsals, which confuses people even more. I bumped into a musician friend of mine while writing this. Musicians often have unique insight into my career, since they, too, deal with gigs, clients, groups, practice, and improvisation. This guy in particular is quite accomplished, a nice guy, and a hometown hero named Darden.

Anyway, he asked what I was doing and I said writing a book on improvisation. He laughed until I thought he was gonna puke. "A BOOK? About improvisation?" Sigh. He's right. But I'm right, too.

Even clients and professional friends kinda know what I do, but not entirely. It took years to learn not to resent the fact that even close friends will see me perform and have a reaction that says, "Oh! *Now*, I get it!" Sigh. In terms of explaining my comedy shows nowadays, I just say that they're funny and interactive.

And I don't advertise. There are two reasons for this. One reason is that I don't like to. The other reason is that I have great clients, so I just do my best to keep helping them. When I see someone who advertises a lot I get suspicious. I think, "What happened to all of your customers? You must get a lot of customers. Don't they come back?" I'm usually busy with repeats and referrals. Yes, I can always use more great clients, but I don't expect to find them through advertising. Consequently, I don't even have a colorful brochure to show Uncle Albert.

I choose to say, "I'm an improviser." Then, when asked what the heck I'm talking about, I choose to say that I am a working comedian and trainer. Some of my comedian friends would disagree when I say I'm a comedian. They'd say I'm a comic actor, not a comedian, because comedians stand there with a mic and tell jokes. I tell them to get a hobby and lighten up.

See? Even the improvisers and stand-up comedians don't always understand what the other does. We share some tools, to be sure, but there are chasms of difference after that. Stand-ups say they'd be scared to try to do what I do. Well, I am scared when I do stand-up comedy. I don't enjoy rehearsed jokes much and stand-ups work alone and drive all the darn time. I don't see a grand prize in that.

See how none of this will help Uncle Albert to have any insight as to what I do for a living? Sometimes I benefit from this anonymity. I tell myself that I am shrouded in mystery. I have wiggle room. This makes me feel that I can take any type of gig I want. I get challenged often and I love winning. The lack of understanding of what I do provides me a great environment for creativity. I don't know what I'm going to do anyway. But I will know. When it is time.

THE IMPROVISED
LIFE

"YOU TOO CAN BE A PROFESSIONAL COMEDIAN!"

As told to the National Comedy Gym Convention...

I jotted three things down on a bevnap a few minutes before I went up to speak and they have served me well ever since. That day I hadn't intended to improvise my speech, I just hadn't thought about needing a written one. This is how it went...

Want to be a professional comedian? I have the three-step process that worked for me.

    1. Get gigs.

    2. Get paid for gigs.

    3. Repeat.

Now there are a lot of smaller, but VERY important steps in between those main steps. Such as, 1a: "Don't suck," which occurs again at 2a and 3a. There are a bunch of other sub-steps we'll talk about later. But these are the big three steps I recommend as a beginning framework. Each step is as important as the next.

Step 1 is important. You can't get anywhere without gigs. Hopefully they are good gigs, but you need gigs in any case: all types of them. Learn from them. Learn where to get them. These answers vary from place to place, situation to situation. Get gigs through your friends as well as from strangers. Give your friends gigs whenever you can.

Step 2 is important. You can't get anywhere without getting paid for gigs. Hopefully it is good pay, but you need to get paid in any case: all types of pay. Learn to deserve good pay. Learn how to get good pay. Learn where to get good pay. These answers vary from place to place, situation to situation.

Step 3 is very important. It's a big one. I don't understand how anyone makes it without Step 3, especially people who market their comedy and training too aggressively. If you have had a bunch of clients and you made them all very happy, wowed their audiences, solved their problems, if you did all these things, then why are you advertising so much? Aren't your hands full with all those past and returning clients who want you back? If you do excellent work you should be able to market more selectively. As for me, I barely market at all. Not for my shows and training, at least. And yet the phone keeps ringing. I like to think that it is because I make good, fun promises to my clients and then leave them very happy. You can't get anywhere without repeating. Hopefully, your best jobs repeat, but you need to repeat in any case: all types of repeating, like a different job for the same client. Learn ways to leave your clients happy.

'KEEP A GOIN'. AND DON'T WORRY ABOUT LITTLE STUFF TOO MUCH AND GET ALL DOWN.'

And never forget…

The Mystery Problem

I love telling people about The Mystery Problem. They will inevitably inquire, "What is The Mystery Problem?" To which

I can reply that, if we knew what The Mystery Problem was, we'd probably have a better name for it, wouldn't we? In the meantime, take it from a veteran that there will often be a Mystery Problem, so don't go promising clients shows and traveling all over by whatever means without allowing time, energy, and equipment as needed to solve the forthcoming Mystery Problem.

I have a relationship with The Mystery Problem. Freshmen are surprised when they meet The Mystery Problem. This could be anything from a bad mic to the room being set-up wrong, to the client having wrong travel times for you. To be a functioning Pro Improviser, always try to anticipate and allow for The Mystery Problem. I arrive early to check the performance room and equipment, and then I take whatever break time is left. More about The Mystery Problem later.

Love It

Above all, don't do it unless you love what you do. There are certainly easier career choices. Many pros are doing it because it's what they have to do. Do it your way and go for it each night. Win each show. And I'll close this with a quote from my wife's ancient and wise Italian Grandfather. He was a prolific stonemason who made many of the finest cast sculptures found in Texas. He kept making stuff until he was older than the stones. Angels in churches, gargoyles on buildings, he made excellent stuff. And he was a happy man. Excellence combined with work you love will do that. He said this about being a happy, excellent pro, "Keep a goin'. And don't worry about little stuff too much and get all down," at which point he would make a face, then laugh and drop a tear—every time. I use that a lot. Then he'd burst into "Che Bella Cosa! La Giornata di en sole!"—while dancing. He had fun for nearly 100 years.

The Third Career

Let me make one thing clear, I am by no means a pioneer in comedy, except where improvisation applies to that. No, comedy is an original job that came with the first inhabitants of our fine planet. Comedy is one of the earliest and most natural of human conditions. Satire, mimicry, and the group laugh are as old as Zugg and Ogg sitting around the fire eating Brontoburgers. It was the third career.

The first career was business. Maybe they had sex to trade for protection, the ability to keep a fire going to trade for meat, meat to trade for access to fire, a club or muscles to claim the best cave with, that sort of thing. These actions became careers like prostitutes, merchants, developers, butchers, bakers, candlestick makers, some teachers, and some bullies.

The second career was leader. Someone in the group, whether good or bad, would stand on a rock or push someone down and declare the next move. "We will hunt over there." "The men will eat first." "This is the right way." That sort of thing. These people became mayors, preachers, bosses, some teachers, and some bullies.

The third career was comedy. While the leader stood on the rock proclaiming, "This is the right way," we stood behind them mimicking them, making faces, saying, "Thees issa da poopie hwaaayee." It was the natural balance and the obvious third career. We comedians have a primary group function and social responsibility that is to call the seriousness of the first two jobs, situations, and life itself into perspective and balance. These careers include comics, cartoonists, satirists, clowns, comedians, angry victims, some teachers, and some bullies.

PLAYS WELL WITH OTHERS

*If you're stressed, lower your
expectations.* — Keith Johnstone

Back to those report cards in elementary school. They typically started with grades and comments regarding reading, then writing and arithmetic, and then the fourth item was usually something similar to "Plays Well With Others." Look how important play is!! It's right up there with the big three! It totally matters and not just for kids. Many of the basic aspects of our personalities don't change from kids to adulthood; the principles of play still matter. If you think that being stuck in the house sick for a week made you grumpy, think what a decade behind a desk might do! Play well with others! Have some fun or you'll creep the rest of us out.

It Still Counts

Playing is a biggie. If you abandon playing, you are getting rustier at interactivity and imagination each day. Your productivity takes a beating. You have less and less fun. It was the only life skill on that report card that doesn't end or get finished. We need to play for life.

It Still Counts

Playing Well With Others wasn't so prominent on your report card by accident. Playing is how we learned our agreement, disagreement, and negotiation skills. It's where we found balance in being nice and not nice. It's where we learned to compete and collaborate.

'JUST LIKE YOUR BODY DIMINISHES WITHOUT EXERCISE, YOUR SPIRIT DIMINISHES WITHOUT PLAY.'

Most of you would never aspire to being a full-time comedian improviser. But you do need to master play in your lives in order to flourish and have personal success that fulfills you. Just like our report cards in school, Playing Well With Others is right up there with the big three of reading, writing, and arithmetic. And for grown-ups, it kind of takes over first place on our report cards. Since most of us read, write, and add about as well as we ever will, we are left with how to live, which is in the Playing Well With Others category. The first three are like white-collar mechanics and Playing Well With Others is like health and love. Without play, there is no context and no success.

Improvisation and play are very closely related. Play is the exercise of the soul. It is the way we know spiritual and life balance. To know the truth through meditation is great but it is only a step towards being the truth in motion. Improvisation is a way to navigate play, a way to ride the waves of everything you know to where it seems best within the play.

Just like your body diminishes without exercise, your spirit diminishes without play. Furthermore, if you don't play your spirit grows awkward in its interaction with other spirits.

Play is an environment of knowing and doing. It values what is between us. It devalues being too judgmental.

Life is a bit like riding a bike in this manner. You don't think about all the component parts while doing it, you just trust yourself to do them. You learn to balance, to peddle; you learn confidence, likelihoods, and desires. You ride. For The Improvised Life we might say you learn to act, to react, to join, support, enjoy, co-create, explore. You play.

Yes, and...

There is a famous saying that comedy comes in threes and I have found that often to be so true. And since the most important takeaway from this book for all of us is the message *Yes and* we will now look at it for the first of three times.

The basic concept that drives improvisational creativity amongst players is usually called *Yes and*. The idea is that an idea or inference is offered and the other player agrees with it by adding something to it. This is beyond acceptance; it is additive. This is the basic fuel that makes improv go so fast and travel so far. To not accept and use ideas would be blocking. This way the outcome is often just as surprising to the players as it is to the viewer. Also, the outcomes are usually more interesting than if one person had driven the moments instead of *Yes anding*, which is how improvisers describe using *Yes and*.

Yes and is the power we knew as kids playing make-believe. We built amazing places and stories effortlessly by building upon each other's ideas. This isn't agreement; it is acceptance and addition. Agreement is passive, but *Yes and* is active. We show agreement in action and it is received the same way and the atomic reaction is off and running. We surprise ourselves and recognize ourselves at the same time.

Yes and extends into how you choose to lead your life. It doesn't free you from the need to judge your commitments, but it certainly does free you from being judgmental. Some of the most exciting sequences of your life will come from saying, *Yes and*. This is a far-reaching truth, friends. Mark my words! This is a guarantee. If you learn the power of the *Yes and* it will change you and present you with bounty.

Business

In business, you can find more personal and team success by using improvisation and play in your life. It strengthens the fabric among those you interact with and it reduces stress. It presents options to you. It helps you to recognize good ideas. To have the power to Play Well With Others in business is to have many advantages. You and your team are faster and more confident. The moment becomes powerful for you over and over again. And it's free, free, free, if you can get it into your life. It ties all together, too. You'll be stronger at work and at home.

Life

Of course, this extends to the rest of your life as well. Family, spouse, friends: who wouldn't like a less stressed, quick-witted, confident you? My dog even likes it when I've been playing well. I'm more fun after a show, for sure.

And you need it. Your life is important and you deserve to have fun. When you are energized with fun and the power of active agreement, your ideas spark. You enjoy the people in your life more. You are more aware of the beauty and options in life that can be seen when one is good *in the moment.*

Let's not forget that humorous, healthy people are sexy, too. You hear it all the time. They have confidence and great circulation. I'm just sayin'...how's that for a perk?

And it is a natural state of the human condition to come up with synergistic solutions and functionality together. Birds fly, fish swim, and humans collaborate and experience buoyant synergy. We are drawn to the power of synergy because it is our innate human power. It is one of the highest powers we can access. It allows us to tap into the higher states of life. God, the perfection of creation, and pure fun are inviting us there constantly.

Lower My Expectations!?
"Uncle Roland and the Potato Salad"

When I was a kid I loved spending time with my Mom's best friend Peggy. I loved her. She loooved me. Peggy was a heck of a gal. She often wrangled her extended family into weekends at the lake, card parties, and all sorts of fun stuff. This is the story of one of those many events. I was about seven years old at the time.

Peggy is having a big dinner at her house. I can't remember the occasion. There might not have been one. But there's a long table and we are all gathering around it starving for Peggy's good Southern cooking. There are her cousins, her sons, her daughter, extended families, maybe even a neighbor or two.

Peggy had a cousin named Roland. Roland was a grown man in his 40s and a twin to his brother Raymond. This was a very fun-loving clan, but Roland was particularly spontaneous and funny to me as a kid. Turned out the man was mildly retarded, as in mentally retarded. As a kid, though, that didn't mean much to me, and I just thought he was very lighthearted and unpredictable. He didn't seem to carry stress. I liked sitting by him, so that's where I went at the table.

Well, Peggy and others were coming out of the kitchen with these big family-portion bowls of salad, corn on the cob, green beans, sweet potatoes, mashed potatoes, potato salad, pinto beans, muffins, butter, bread, platters of steaks, grilled chicken and sausages, big pitchers of sweet tea, and we all knew there were pies in the kitchen, too. Everything was being placed on the table and Peggy put a huge family-size bowl of potato salad down in front of Roland. This bowl was a foot high and a foot in diameter filled with thick, creamy, homemade, potato salad.

Roland was saying something fun to me when he saw the potato salad land. He looked at it, looked at me, then pulled it over a little closer to himself and started eating. Right out of the bowl. With the big serving spoon. He ate and ate. I thought he was so irreverent and funny. Quiet, too, he wasn't hamming it up. He kept eating. Now I was impressed for other reasons. Roland was wasting no time. He must have eaten several pounds of potato salad when he began whimpering. A pound later he was quietly crying, still eating. He was as full of potato salad as a man can be, but he was maintaining his pace anyway. I stared in smirking awe and disbelief.

Peggy comes back by dropping more platters of something off and sees Roland crying and working that over-sized spoon to the bottom of the potato salad bowl. She exclaimed with concern for the man, "Roland! Oh, my God! What are you doing!?"

Roland looks up at her sobbing, still chewing potato salad, but slowing considerably. He says to her with love and apology in his eyes, "I'm sorry, Peggy, but I just don't think I can eat this whole thing."

Now, no one told Roland to eat that potato salad poundage. He chose it to be his cross to bear, his dragon to slay, his windmill. I tell the story here because I see so much of this phenomenon in work teams. People have chosen all sorts of insurmountable tasks to burden themselves with. We set our watches fast so we might trick ourselves into being on time. We work on weekends to catch-up with excessive promises of productivity, and often weaken the product in many cases because of it.

> "IF YOU ARE EXCESSIVELY STRESSED AND DOING YOUR BEST, THEN CONSIDER LOWERING YOUR EXPECTATIONS AND CONTINUE DOING YOUR BEST. IT IS A SIGN OF INTELLIGENCE, NOT WEAKNESS."

It took me a long time to accept what Keith Johnstone says in the quote at the beginning of this chapter, but it's true. Excessive self-burdening is a choice. If you are a good person doing your best, then excessive expectations can only take you out of your prime mode. If you are excessively stressed and doing your best, then consider lowering your expectations and continue doing your best. It is a sign of intelligence, not weakness. You are doing your best either way.

You don't have to eat all that potato salad. You'd have a better meal if you lowered your potato salad expectations and left room for some diversity in the meal.

CHAPTER 7

THE IMPROVISED LIFE

All men are caught in an inescapable network of mutuality. — Martin Luther King Jr.

The improvised life is living engaged with the rest of concurrent creation. It is a value system driven by obvious truths in the moment. One of the truths of the moment is that we are all connected. Another truth in the moment is that our choices in life have profound effects on others. Why do we limit others and ourselves with diminished views of the opportunities and beauty of the human condition? *We* are the ones who assign value to each other. We have that choice. It should be high, shouldn't it?

The Improvised Life. The adventure, surprise, and incredible productivity of living in the moment: this is how to be fully engaged in the wonders of life. I intend to strike light into the darkness of those who dismiss the moment as unproductive and instead apply themselves to ego-riddled intellectual processes. I say, "Live in the moment, alone and together." We are all alone and together. We should play nice.

Humor

So, I make my living with improvisation. I don't only mean I make my income that way. I stay in improvisational mode much of the time. It's a way to enjoy the people and textures in your life. It's a way to make decisions, manage concerns, and have great funny fun. It uses humor. Even if you aren't into comedy you'd better be into humor. Humor is more like mood. It is a receptiveness to fun and playful occurrences and a lightness of attitude. Humor and improv go hand in hand.

The Moment

In the moment. By working in the moment I have had some incredible outcomes. I would go further to say that...

In the moment, you are sitting at the crossroads of everything. The universe can be seen and you are at the confluence of not only everything you ever learned, thought, intended, but also where you are going and all your opportunities are awaiting in that moment. Anything that keeps part of you out of the moment diminishes your opportunities in the moment. That is to say, preconception and concern for outcome hamstring your potentialities in the moment.

That's tragic, because creativity happens and decisions are made in the moment.

Some Type A personalities have a very difficult time accepting this. They have already chosen some skill sets that they work aggressively to achieve an acceptable, even proud level of productivity. In so doing, they immensely disrespect not only others' potentialities, but their own.

Consider this. You might be able to learn, design, plan, prepare, execute, manage, create, and exhibit a host of other fine skills, but if you can agree that our world has infinite possibilities, then you must admit that one can only scratch the surface of true potentiality without the ability to flourish in the moment. You may be very good at running your particular racehorses, but they'll never amount to more than a fraction of the potentialities. Or look at it this way, create the best list of skills that you can and realize that improvising turns those assets into a synergistic team. It's almost like applying the concept of group mind to your separate skills, but more on that later.

Respect

The moment is inhabited by ultimate respect—respect for others, for self, and for all creation and how it magnificently provides for us. An inability to flourish in the moment is full of disrespect for all the same things.

The improvised life lives in the moment and spins off gifts born out of respect, love, and ultimate potentialities. A disregard for the moment breeds insecurity, distrust, and unhappiness.

Living a life full of disregard may yield things like possessions and titles, but they are hollow possessions that don't offer true success. I'm not against the cool things in this world. On the contrary, I like cool things. But true

"THE IMPROVISED LIFE LIVES IN THE MOMENT AND SPINS OFF GIFTS BORN OUT OF RESPECT, LOVE, AND ULTIMATE POTENTIALITIES."

success is personal and taps into the infinite, whereas anything else will eventually be beside the point. True success is a unique formula in that it works for that individual first and foremost. Like a recipe, it is a combination that works; it is a balance, a flavor, and these things can be known only through the moment. It works for you or it doesn't.

Loving Your Collaborators

It is you who decides if your collaborators' input is brilliant or dumb. We often hold the key to others success in this way, with a simple belief system. One of my favorite quotes that explains to me the fabric of humanity and our hopes and desires within it is the quote from Martin Luther King Jr. that started this chapter. To me it is a quote about engaging fully and attaining the exponential benefits to all of us if we will Play Well With Others and take this human condition to where it can go. MLK couldn't have known that I would see his words as a trumpeting call for improvisation in life. But I know we are describing the same mechanism in humanity: the agreement, empowerment, and fulfillment of a great game where we all feel the deep satisfaction and success of the play.

The great MLK said it like this…

I cannot be what I ought to be until you are what you ought to be. You cannot be what you ought to be until I am what I ought to be.

All the best games start with some premise of fairness. All great games allow for greatness to occur to all players engaged in the game. And the best game of all is the human condition. We were made to play joyously in this game. Like most games, it only works to its fullest potential if all players are engaged.

CHAPTER 8

NOW AND FOREVER

Stay centered by accepting whatever you are
doing. This is the ultimate. — Chuang Tzu

It's interesting to note that etymologically the word spirituality comes from breath, which is not only the basis of most of what we know, but also one of the first and most important instructions to babies, actors, patients, athletes, meditators; you name it. Breathe.

Spirituality and the Moment

Most of us find spirituality in the moment, be it prayer, meditation, appreciation of creation, or other conduits.

In improvisation relevant to spirituality, much can be found vis-à-vis music and technology. Superlatives come up immediately when you cast about for characters in this conversation. Right off, I think of John Coltrane, sainted by some and with his own religious following, and Ray Kurzweil, considered by many to be the heir to Einstein in futuristic thought.

Much has been written about improvisation and spirituality by musicians and artists, scientists, and experts in many different religions.

Consider...

The moment is the most potent source of creativity and productivity.

Productivity and creativity are almost identical, except that productivity is applied creativity.

Improvisation is a skill set that helps to live in and flourish in the moment.

The moment and spirituality are almost identical; therefore, improvisation is applied spirituality.

Close cousins of improv in this sense are prayer, song, dance, love, creativity in general, potentiality, and productivity, especially when applied by more than one being at a time.

Life, including family, recreation, and business, thrives on the *applied* moment and the *doing* of improvisation. This *doing* is particularly important to the modern mind-set. We need to *do* and *apply*. We are not built to worship purely in thought or daydream into universality. Even the Bible says that what you DO counts. The Improvised Life is something you DO.

If improvisation is spiritual, then the act of improvising is the practice of faith. When improvising, you are showing your faith in the unshakeable perfection of creation. When improvising joyfully, you are reveling in God's creation. It can be a window to God in the same way that music, art, and nature are, that is, if you are a person looking for windows to God. It brings you closer to God, nature, each other, and yourself. I have seen it enrich and embolden many lives this way. It strengthens people's lives, relationships, optimism, and peace of mind. In some cases, I've seen improvisation over time transform pinch-faced, distracted souls into more realized and peaceful people. As an example, there have been a handful of marriages started in my company. All are still going strong. Take that, damn divorce rate!

Ease and Creativity

Leading an improvised life isn't work; it's ease. Flourishing in the moment and spinning off creativity and productivity of any type is a natural human condition. Many unhappy people are unhappy for the simple reason that they don't have creativity in their lives. If birds were meant to fly and fish were meant to swim, then humans were meant to co-create, to tap into the moment together and flourish in a way that nothing else we know of can. This was true when Zugg and Ogg created ways to survive and it's true today as we begin to cure cancers. It's a natural state of being human. It isn't work; it's ease.

"WHEN IMPROVISING, YOU ARE SHOWING YOUR FAITH IN THE UNSHAKEABLE PERFECTION OF CREATION. WHEN IMPROVISING JOYFULLY, YOU ARE REVELING IN GOD'S CREATION."

When an improvised thing happens and it was highly effective, we can't take that much credit for it sometimes. You certainly don't want to stare at it. In improv we have a saying, "It went the way it was supposed to go." There is a certain amount of *allowing* creativity and improvisation to offer up great ideas *through us* rather than *of us*.

Improvisation and the New

Both from curiosity and entrepreneurially, one can ask where the *new* comes from. The new idea or application tends to come out of the moment. Diligence and process can further and develop ideas, but the new comes in the moment, where interdisciplinary thought occurs. For instance, life change can be fueled by new thought and improvisation welcomes new thought in the moment. It enables adaptation in that way. An example of this in business might be the drug company coming up with a better blood pressure medication and turning it into Viagra. Yowza! That was *new* and a huge wealth builder. Probably improved some personal lives, too. Snicker...

In life and business, improvisation is a gateway not only to creativity and productivity, but also to greatness, innovation, rejuvenation, profit, and success. According to many futurists, improvisation will be the most important skill in using emerging technologies, such as creativity augmentation, to any advantage. In a world of quickening change, improvisation fits the human condition. Education, preparation, and improvisation are the true security in the future. With these we can adapt and do what is best.

CHAPTER 9

HOW TO FEEL JOY, OPPORTUNITY, PEACE, AND SUCCESS

One must be fond of people and trust them if one is not to make a mess of life. — E.M. Forster

Everything is a manifestation of the human condition.

When I was in acting school we had to learn the concept of dramatic action. In a way, dramatic action is what a person is really doing. It often reveals the underlying relationship or need. For instance, the action might be to show someone a photo album, but the true dramatic action might very well be that the person is pleading not to be left alone. That would be a dramatic action. Like a couple that is arguing. There is some act such as to accuse, defend, destroy, scare, plead, demand, whatever, but the argument would just be a manifestation of the dramatic action, a detail but not the thing that is real. The need, love, hate, aversion, attraction, respect, destruction, these things are closer to the real. Notice that they are all verbs? It is in motion, it is what we do; it's not what we reason out. And it's certainly not the objects and items of this world; it is us who made them alternately valuable or not valuable in the first place. Object value is transient. We assign different values to different things in a manifestation of our true acts.

Humans are consistently perplexed with how to flourish within the human condition. Mainly this is because we are surrounded by objects; impressed by appearances, strictly reactive to surfaces, and we too often mistake these material things for the real things that are important for us as humans. We don't see the stuff in between objects, in between things, in between living creatures, especially humans. We often slide into seeing things backwards.

We feel or don't feel joy. We are inspired or not. We find or don't find love. Yet instead of knowing joy, inspiration, and love, we see activities, objects, and individuals. The truth is that the things that describe the human condition are everything BUT those things, or any "thing" else. We are most affected by the fabric that holds all things we know of in context. The fabric of our lives, of our very existence, the stuff around us everywhere—all the elements of our world are defined by our connected humanity, our essential reality of connectedness. It is because of this fabric that everything else has value or not.

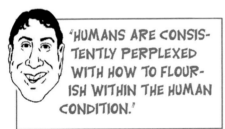

"HUMANS ARE CONSISTENTLY PERPLEXED WITH HOW TO FLOURISH WITHIN THE HUMAN CONDITION."

Confidence and Trust

Usually it is not the object but how you see it, not the thing but how you feel about the thing. And we are all in it together. This is a grand improvisation in motion. In action. We have choices about each other. We can accept, trust, and build upon each other's actions or not. Many of us have been burnt, but so what? How do you want to live? We need you in this.

There are so many gifts for you. Your friends, neighbors, and strangers carry many of these gifts. If you are ready for them, you will find these gifts in the moment. They are free gifts that hold a lot of joy, opportunity, peace, and success.

It is virtually impossible to be trusted if you don't trust. And it is virtually impossible to have lasting confidence without trust, since no one is alone. Improvisation is framed by trust and confidence. It's the way strong choices are related. The adventure is impossible without trust and confidence.

> *If you get down and you quarrel everyday,*
> *You're saying prayers to the devils, I say.*
> *Why not help one another on the way?*
> *Make it much easier.*

— Bob Marley, attributed to Vincent Ford

CHAPTER 10

CAN YOU PROVE IT?

Yes — John Lennon reading Yoko Ono's word on a ladder.

Adages and theories abound as to the benefits of humor in our lives. I've devoted sections in this chapter to some categories of benefits from improvisation and humor that I know to be true, benefits I have measured or tested. Yeah, you heard me. I measure and test sometimes.

First of all, people love improvised humor. Like people love books, or yoga, or walks, or visits with their favorite friends; people love it that much. Many people find that it gives them what they want, even though what they want varies wildly.

There's a lot of data on health benefits from an improvised life with humor. There's a lot of data, some of it generated by me, on business benefits from improvisation and humor. But the big deal to me is what it does for the quality of life of those who love it. I've seen so many different personalities thrive once they'd found a format for working out their play issues. Not just troubled personalities but brilliant ones, and every other flavor as well. Improvisation changes lives. And it's the gift that keeps on giving since it strengthens our life skills in some basic ways. It enables us to have poise and a laugh for free to be found anywhere.

Humor

To be a happy human you've got to have good humor. Even if you aren't into comedy, you'd better be into humor. As I mentioned earlier, humor is more like mood. It is a receptiveness to fun and playful occurrences and a lightness of attitude. Humor and improv go hand in hand, but they are not the same thing.

In improvisation training we often have to remind players not to try to be funny. It doesn't help anything. At the same time, if something funny comes up, develop it and have fun, but don't try or you chase the humor away. This concept applies elsewhere. I want my carpenter to have good humor, but I kind of hope he isn't too much into comedy. I can say the same of my banker, my grocer, etc. We don't always want comedy, especially the contrived kind, but an awareness and receptiveness of positive occurrences and a light attitude can be staples of your life.

So comedy and humor are related but different.

Humor and Health

A cheerful heart is good medicine. — Proverbs 17:22

There is wide agreement that humor is good for health. So is laughter and lowered stress levels. Scientists take turns proving this in different ways over and over again. Some focus on how laughter reduces blood pressure or increases circulation. Others talk about increases in oxygen and good hormones and a reduction in bad hormones. This is proven many times over by now.

In the therapeutic and education worlds, improvisation had been a tool used for decades before it impacted the entertainment and business worlds. One exception to this is jazz, as

I wrote earlier. But those guys were way ahead of their time in investigating the relationships between preparation and improvisation, between creativity and productivity. They also were way ahead of the times investigating the windows between theme and variation and the doorways improvisation opened to soulfulness.

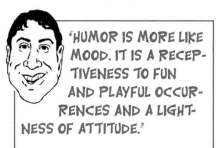

'HUMOR IS MORE LIKE MOOD. IT IS A RECEPTIVENESS TO FUN AND PLAYFUL OCCURRENCES AND A LIGHTNESS OF ATTITUDE.'

They're all correct. But there's more. Improvisation repairs us by getting to the fabric of our lives in the form of human interaction. The improved circulation in our bodies is just a microcosmic example of the circulation we engage in. We joyfully work out our human interactions circulating with like-intentioned people. The result is flow and interest that goes where it should naturally go.

Veteran players will share with each other how they play even when they feel ill. The knee-jerk reaction when sick is to skip the show if possible. We might think that it will be a bad audience experience if we're ill, or our voices will sound bad, or whatever. But veterans know better. Playing when ill often has surprising and wonderful results! You have a freshness of perspective; there's variety in your choices. And while performing, you feel well. I'm not joking; it's like temporary medicine. A veteran improv comedian is likely to look forward to shows when ill.

4 Out of 5 Doctors

(That was a fine comedy-group name.)

Here are some examples from the medical and science community that describe some aspects of the relationship between humor and health.

In an article from the May 1995 issue of *Commerce Now*, Randy Erickson wrote about several studies on humor and health. In that article, entitled "Help for the 'Humor-Impaired,'" he wrote, "It is by now common knowledge that health studies bear out the old adage that laughter is the best medicine. A good belly laugh will lower the blood pressure below normal resting rates for 45 minutes and laughing exercises the lungs, increases oxygen in the bloodstream, and stimulates production of endorphins, the brain's built-in painkiller."

In a nutshell, that's the sort of stuff scientific studies have come up with over and over again, proving what we already believe. But before you start to think that it's all rosy, read on from the same article.

Mr. Erickson goes on to tell us "an astounding fact; preschool children laugh or smile 400 times a day, but that figure drops to an average of only 15 laughs a day by the time people reach age 35." That's how drastic our cases are as grown-ups! That's why the fourth most important thing on our report cards can't go untended into adulthood.

This type of data is borne out elsewhere. Rob Stein of the *Washington Post* reported on a study published in the December 1989 issue of the *American Journal of Medical Science* by Lee Berk, Ph.D., a pathology professor at Loma Linda University in California. Berk showed one group stressful film clips and another group funny film clips. The study compared the participants' reactions. Mr. Stein reported that overall, in the 20 men and women tested, "blood flow decreased by about 35 percent after experiencing stress but increased 22 percent after laughter—an improvement equivalent to that produced by a 15 to 30-minute workout." He also notes there were "significant reductions in stress hormones and enhanced immune function" in the funny film clip group.

Dr. Berk goes on to say, "Laughter is not dissimilar from exercise. It's not going to cure someone from stage three cancer, but in terms of prevention it does make sense. Positive emotions such as laughter affect your biology."

That's not to say that improvisation and play have no role in fighting illness. I have given trainings to several oncology organizations and these people have an acute understanding of this.

Closer to home, I have a friend who was my improvisation teammate for years. Donna is a fun player who is exceptionally well read and full of smart references and musical skills. Tireless in her pursuits, she's a real pro. And the closest friend I've known with cancer.

Improv changed my life. Cheesy statement, yes, but true. I've used the skills I've learned from the world of improv to land a job, enjoy a vacation, and deal with the day-at-a-time trials of cancer. My awareness is sharpened, I know how to truly listen, and I can bring joy to any, absolutely any, situation. The wisdom of the great and mighty "Yes, and" should be learned by all. Seriously, I wouldn't have made it through all the trials of that without the thinking I learned from Les and the people of ComedySportz.

— Donna Kay Yarborough

Well, that's just huge, isn't it? Not bad for just having a laugh. It's like getting several good things at once while doing something you prefer anyway. Multiple benefits are a sign of the improvised life, remember? Reduction in stress has specific benefits, but to really get the good humor health benefits, you need positive humor experiences. It's not enough to limit the bad; you need doses of the good.

For all these reasons and more, doctors concur that there is an association between state of mind and health, especially cardiovascular health. I need to add one more expert opinion in here. I was very influenced by the amount of joy in the life of my wife's grandfather, Vincenzo "Jimmie" Palmieri. In his nineties and only recently retired from the dancing social scene, he was often asked what his secret was for happy longevity. He had this to say on the matter: "Lotta people go around all day like unh (makes exaggerated sad face, bitchy mumbling) and you can't do that. You gotta get going (usually about now he'd leap up beaming a smile, shake his old man arms and do a step, inevitably followed by a bellowed song like that "Che bella cosa!" number I mentioned earlier). Life is pretty damn good."

In my experience, some people of the Mediterranean, especially the Italians, have a short route to fun just like kids do. Doctors are trying to figure that out, too.

Humor and Productivity

Humor can bolster your productivity and improve your bottom line in business and in life.

Here's a good piece of data to start with. This is, again, from Randy Erickson, as published in the May 1995 issue of *Commerce Now.*

"Laughter is good for the health of a business, too, according to University of Wisconsin-La Crosse professor Stu Robertshaw, also known as 'Dr. Humor,' and there have been at least a few studies that bear this out. Robertshaw noted that one corporate study showed that after a trial period during which humor was incorporated into the workplace in a variety of ways—including everything from a special humor bulletin board to silly hat days—the company experienced a 21 percent decrease in staff turnover and a 38 percent decrease in Friday absenteeism."

"A DECREASE IN TURNOVER AND ABSENTEEISM IS PREDICTABLE FROM A WELL-TARGETED AND EXECUTED TRAINING PLAN USING IMPROVISATION."

I agree wholeheartedly. I've tracked this as a gauge of effectiveness myself. In my work I have measured the impact of my improvisational training in ways that can describe a company's bottom line. A decrease in turnover and absenteeism is predictable from a well-targeted and executed training plan using improvisation. In almost every industry, there is a way to responsibly gauge effectiveness. Some things work most of the time, all things work some of the time, and a professional consultant applies the right techniques in the right doses. Your training goals often tie directly into the business operations. Those are often measurable. This sometimes must be solved specifically and uniquely for a particular business.

Additionally, I've had good luck in measuring improvements in recruitment, reductions in insurance claims, reductions in sick days taken, reductions in staff complaints, and the all-encompassing key word: productivity. And, of course, my programs are data-proven successful through many softer types of metrics such as pre-surveys and exit surveys, ongoing feedback, and requests for repeat trainings.

Productivity is a big one. It is impacted by many of the above listed factors. It can be measured many different ways.

In the article "Friendlier Workers More Productive," from the *Journal of Personality and Social Psychology* (August 2003), Cheyenne Hopkins describes a study done at the University of Michigan, and internationally, by psychologist Jeffrey Sanchez-Burks.

"Friendly workers pay attention to indirect meanings, work well with other cultures and are perceived as trustworthy," Sanchez-Burks said. "An impersonal style blinds workers from noticing differences in style. They often fail to notice nonverbal communication."

"What is literally said will be followed closely, but information about the context in which the information is conveyed—information often critical for task success and productivity—is lost," he added. "This type of miscommunication, like ships passing in the night, is further exacerbated in diverse organizations (domestically and internationally) because rarely are people with other cultural backgrounds as impersonal as mainstream Americans."

Ouch, ya know? But I know it to be true.

In my work, I use some different language to describe it. I often use the language of play, like playing catch with balls and issues of passing and continuing as models for communication. But whatever you call it, if you have it, things get better, and if you don't, things get worse.

What Your Team Really Wants

Don't be distracted by the belief that more money makes a team happier or better. Welcome the truth that a team with a cultivated, appropriate sense of community and good improvisation skills can HUGELY impact the bottom line.

This is a quote from Betsy Morris, excerpted from her article "Genentech: The Best Place to Work Now," as printed in *Fortune, 100 Best Companies To Work For And Why 2006.*

> *For starters, most of the things that make a workplace great turn out to cost employers absolutely nothing. Next, a great workplace benefits more than just employees: Over the past five years the stocks of the four companies I worked at trounced the market, up a compounded 24 percent vs. the S&P's 1 percent gain.*

I have found this to be true in my own survey work. I did a series of surveys where I asked the question, "Why do you go to work?" I did another series of surveys that asked the question, "What would make your job better?"

I surveyed sample groups with my associate Terrill Fisher when we were partners in Humor University. I also surveyed and interviewed groups on my own in some government agencies, schools, and companies. When asked the question, "Why do you go to work?" money is often cited initially when the question was asked in front of teammates, but when committing to priorities, when reaching consensus in the group, and when asked in private, individuals rarely had money as their second priority and almost never had it as their first. Their first priority, across the board, in every industry, was a comment on the work community and their identity within it. Some representative comments were, "Because my coworkers are expecting me" and "It wouldn't be fair to make my coworkers cover my duties; I need to hold up my end of the bargain" and "Because it's what I do." These are all issues of community.

In one case, I was hired to assess a group's needs and design an improvisational training program to treat any problems. It was no secret that morale was low. The bosses had just given financial bonuses company-wide and to thousands of employees to try and improve the team's morale. Morale plummeted. Money hadn't been the problem and even worse the employees were a little insulted and disheartened by the boss's lack of communication and vision on the matter. I'm not saying the employees had never asked for, even asked vociferously for, more money in "public," I'm just saying it was apples and oranges in regards to what they truly needed. When I reported my findings to the bosses there was anger and frustration in the room, as you might expect after releasing huge amounts of funds and being off-target. The employees didn't really want money after all; they wanted improved communication processes (especially an improvement in how bosses listened to what the employees had to say), and meaningful and accurate recognition for accomplishments. The bosses had major confusion as to how this could be true.

When asked, "What would make your job better?" the main answer is usually support. People want to feel that if they are making a valuable enough contribution to a company that they will be supported. Such support takes different forms, but it is often the correct framing and sustenance of support that makes people's jobs better. In many of the survey responses this form of support was generally referred to as, "Respect for their contribution."

The Group Mind

Birds do it. Bees do it. — Cole Porter

There is a lot written and a lot of research done on concepts of the group mind. Just about everyone agrees with its existence and some of its properties, but the agreement kinda stops there. I am quite familiar with it and I usually call it group mind or GSS for Group Synergy and Service. While it is an effect of almost all my work, I rarely explain it to clients.

Basically the concept is that we can achieve a state of synergy, resonance, and attunement in a group that enables a different form of thought that is made up of the group mind instead of the individual minds.

In some ways, improvisation and play are access points to the group mind. This is a big deal. The group mind is capable of amazing effects that range from super-creativity to health benefits.

The group mind is a concept that has caused much discussion over the last few decades. Too many of us have experienced it for its existence to be in doubt, but scientists have tried to nail down the phenomenon with only limited success. There are multiple concepts fueled by group mind theory. There's Collective Wisdom, Collective Consciousness, Teamwork, Creativity, Group Service, etc.

Companies and small groups of all types, from intentional communities to support groups to families, are hungry to cultivate it and benefit from it. Other groups might be small like project teams or large ones like movements. While most of us have some amount of experience with it, relatively few of us know how to create it, or even know what the parameters of its existence are.

Basically it goes like this...

Groups of people with a commitment to dropped preconceptions, shared creativity, clear goals, and a cultivated sense of purposeful support of each other can achieve higher forms of synergy that have major positive outcomes.

The process includes structured play, sacred space (a private space and the agreement that it will be constructive and nonjudgmental), repetition, communion, shared goals, and a deep appreciation of synergistic relationships. The creativity and productivity can be absolutely profound.

Most of us have had some experience with this truth. I hear it from soldiers who served together under pressure. I hear it from nurse teams. I hear it from groups of college friends, casts of plays, and intense project development teams.

Improvisers have talked about it for years. The early, long-form, improv technique "Harold" was roughly based on conjuring up the group mind. When it happens the improvisers describe "seeing Harold." The improv pioneer Del Close was heavily identified with this movement.

Group mind can be created most easily in groups of eight or so. In some cases, it gets created in entire movements. Meditators are waiting for it to hit critical mass on a large scale and change the world with Cosmic Consciousness. Evolutionists say it is happening over multiple generations: that we are getting nicer, more cooperative, and closer to concepts of group attunement.

Improvisers who play together have easier access to this phenomenon. We cultivate it and experience it regularly and purposefully. I can build it in hours, even with novices; but to sustain it requires practice in a group setting.

A cultivated community with GSS can access deeper levels of change and growth. The difference is short-term vs. long-term. It is like the difference between communion during the process of falling in love and the communion cultivated in a long-term married relationship. We fall in love with our group's flavor of GSS over time and conjuring it up can become very functional and easier to maintain because it becomes a lasting value.

"IF NOTHING ELSE, THE GROUP MIND FEELS GREAT TO HUMANS. IT DEFINES OUR COMMUNITY. IT GIVES US HEALTH AND CONFIDENCE."

Some of this is done with play and the ritual of practice; some by instilling a correct cultural environment that allows the necessary values to grow. Play and improvisation achieve both of these aspects naturally through a value system of creativity, trust, synergy, make-believe (or, more accurately, to make belief), and by going to the well on a regular basis to support all of these values.

The payoff is immense. A group with the power to develop group mind is capable of much more than the talents of its component parts. We've all seen it happen in the crucible of emergencies, deadlines, etc. It isn't for panic and emergency only though. It can be used freely and purposefully, if it is cultivated. Over time it becomes easier and easier, and going back to the loneliness and lack of synergy that preceded it becomes an archaic, counter-productive concept. Who would plod when they can soar with less effort?

So I build group mind. While it is confusing and elusive to many, it is a tool of the trade in upper-level improvisation. And we're not the only ones. Historically, groups of hunters practice dance and ritual before a hunt in order to attune and build resonance. They are reminding each other of their bond of trust and synergy through the ritual of practice. The famous Blue Angels do a quiet spoken ritual that reviews all moves before they take to the air to do their incredibly integrated teamwork flying. (Project teams in business gravitate this way with retreats and regular meetings, but they are only drawn to the concepts; they are not truly cultivating them.) Championship teams in sports are an example of synergistic ritual in practice. They are operating under group mind and GSS. We see it all around us.

Audience members and workshop participants sometimes struggle to name the phenomenon when they see us use it. They call it clairvoyance or accuse us of a hidden language. They are close, but it is easier than they imagine and they could have it, too, if they were to have it correctly cultivated over time.

Here is the big deal when it comes to group mind. It is natural and we are drawn to it and its power. Earlier in this book I referred to a set of studies I did based on the question, "Why do you go to work?" I described that the top answers were about community, identity, responsibility, etc. In truth, it is the amazing drawing power of GSS that is the glue of most groups with shared goals. We smell it even if we don't get to feast on it and it keeps us going to the well. It is what makes us band together. It is a way to know the power we have.

I read recently that ants get more aggressive if they are part of a community. They send a message to the other ants like, "Lookout, I'm in a big group with synergy and they got my back." Even though the other ants see only the solo ant, they revere his confidence and can see that he has the power of GSS.

Other animals show us insight into the group mind as well, such as birds and fish. When a flock of birds in flight all change directions purposefully and spontaneously in unison there was either a variable leader or no leader at all. It is the same with a school of fish or migrating buffalo or a pack of wolves. It is a natural state, one in which humans are perhaps the greatest example, yet we barely use it outside of play and emergencies.

If nothing else, the group mind feels great to humans. It defines our community. It gives us health and confidence. And it can be scary powerful to the unpracticed.

The Federal Judges and Airborne Group Mind

When groups experience play and GSS for the first time in a long while, they can get a little overwhelmed with happiness and spunk. This is the story of how I learned to remind everyone of safety before each and every workshop.

The federal judges of the Fifth Circuit Court of Appeals hired me for a half-day improvisation workshop on teambuilding, communication skills, and stress relief at the lovely

Horseshoe Bay Conference Center, a place I had used many times before.

I was warned that they were older and stodgy and it might be tough. I've gotten *warnings* lots of times and they usually don't affect me. This time was no exception. I found them willing. Once they saw that I knew what I was doing and they were having fun, things started getting energetic. There were about 30 or 40 participants, so it even got a little loud.

I was assisted by Terrill Fischer, friend and fellow performer in my company. We were having a great day and everyone was engaged. There were little eruptions of group mind occurring and they were getting jazzed about it. Eventually, I got to a game I wanted to play with them called, "EVERYBODY GO!"

"I CAN'T HELP BUT WONDER HOW MUCH TROUBLE ONE GETS INTO FOR KILLING AN ENTIRE CIRCUIT OF FEDERAL JUDGES."

For that game we all stand in a circle. One participant steps forward and says, "Everybody go..." and then does something. The group all says, "Yes!" together and then we all do that same thing. Well, they were getting into it and some were a bit delirious with laughter. It was a sight to see all those distinguished white-haired individuals playing their judicious butts off.

So, I'm standing by a judge as his turn comes up and he yells, "Everybody go..." He glances at me as he sets himself into motion and with the group mind thing going on I feel his thoughts and his physicality and then adrenaline shoots into my veins.

Switch to extreme slow motion.

This older gentleman is leaping up into the air. Not a hop or a jump but a full-fledged, gravity-defying leap. In a flash I realize I didn't tell them they couldn't kill themselves or anyone else. People get unpredictable sometimes when you turn them on to the energy of play that they'd left behind at some point. They were ready to say *Yes and* to any darn thing I let occur.

My mind is white hot with possibilities. He is in mid-air and starting to flip over. He is *flipping over.* My muscles all clench as I realize he is tossing his brittle body into a headfirst, hip-hop snaking dive maneuver on the hard floor. His eyes are wild with childish challenge and glee. His open-mouthed grin is barely contained by his silver beard.

Terrill and I dive to throw ourselves between this old federale and the unyielding earth. I'm diving with my hands out flat trying to get them between the guy's head and floor before impact. I may not be able to save him from a broken neck and concussion but at least I can try to save his life. His eyes are gleaming and show no fear whatsoever. I wonder what happens when a federal judge kills himself doing an improv exercise in front of all his fellow justices.

Oh, my GOD! The other judges!!! By the time I think it, the air is split with the exuberant yelled response of "Yes!" from the other judges. They are thrilled and eager to comply with his charge and they are all beginning to leap in the air and flip over to headfirst position! Terrill and I are screaming and reaching in all directions. I can't help but wonder how much trouble one gets into for killing an entire circuit of federal judges. Bye-bye, home and family. I killed federal judges in a state that is over productive in executions.

Thankfully the instigator is unscathed. The rest of them were stopped in the nick of time still able to land on their feet. They are looking at the now apoplectic me and I am reeling with the group mind flashing in my head. They think they won. What, I don't know, but they have the gleam of bad kids in their eyes and they are oddly proud.

The power of play and group mind is huge and can be danger-ous in the hands of someone who knows how to get groups to that point but doesn't have the experience to manage it proactively. It is a palpable power. Not vague or mystic or new age-y. I have NEVER missed safety admonishments since.

ESPECIALLY with groups I've been warned might not "get into it." The bigger they are, the harder they fall and you gotta be intuitive and careful.

In the old days I sure could have used a handbook...

THE HANDBOOK FOR AN IMPROVISED LIFE

CHAPTER 11

READY TO PLAY IMPROV?

This time like all times is a very good one if we but know what to do with it. — Ralph Waldo Emerson

The good news is that anybody and everybody can improvise. You improvise all the time, do you realize that? Some examples of important improvisations you do regularly are driving, answering the phone, and responding to an unplanned event or opportunity. Important stuff, huh? You also improvise partially or completely when you do anything for the first time, which I guess is just about anything you've ever done. Improvisational moments define your entire life if you look at it this way.

When you ask a roomful of people if they improvise, or if they improvise at work, some say, "No." Sometimes it's more than some. The denial! My heart goes out to them. If more of us practice play and improvisation, stress will go down, productivity will go up, people will be healthier and happier—and more attractive, I might add. We'll have a funner tomorrow.

If you have never practiced or studied improvisation, then you mainly improvise by instinct. Instincts and instinctive action are developed and exercised while playing. These instinctual skills empower your other skills of organization and preparation, planning, and managing, etc. Improvisational skills value your preparation, but also show you doorways and combinations that illuminate opportunities as they swirl about, unseen by rigid thinkers.

Let's take a world champion basketball team for an example. There is no denying the organizational and preparation skills necessary to get them to the brink of championship. But likewise there is no denying the next level of play they achieve, which is intensely improvisational, instinctual, *full* of electric play, and group mind.

This state of synergistic and exciting flow exhibited by champion team players shows us a way to access our utmost interests and the unfettered electricity of life. This is the state of mind we intend to learn about. You need to know it about yourself. You deserve the flashes of focused imagination and glimpses of alternative angles, empowering combinations, and outright pleasant surprises.

"YOU DESERVE THE FLASHES OF FOCUSED IMAGINATION AND GLIMPSES OF ALTERNATIVE ANGLES, EMPOWERING COMBINATIONS, AND OUTRIGHT PLEASANT SURPRISES."

Anybody can learn to improvise and enjoy it and recapture the sense of play they had as a child. I've seen it done by the rich and the poor, executives, programmers, bankers, accountants, manufacturers, plumbers, supervisors, office staff, probates, and judges, and even the occasional self-absorbed actor, to name a few. Virtually everybody loves it. Some study only a few levels. Some think about becoming performers. Many are so hooked they go pro or semi-pro. Almost all of them have day jobs that benefit from their improvisation.

And it is a blast and a hoot and a darn fun time. People are always telling me that improvisation makes them feel more like themselves. They remember things they like about themselves and others. They are reminded that they are quick-witted and strong and fun. People also tell me that other people like them better. It might be that they've dropped some stress and recovered their positive attitude and a smile. Smiling can show you in a whole new light and it is a fine thing to be seen in a new light.

Some more good news is that it is often free or cheap to learn and practice improvisation. There are improvisation groups and training centers in every major city in the world nowadays. I'll tell you where some of the good ones are and what they're like.

This book is where to start, of course. Share yours with your friends. Give them the message to have more fun and do better. If you get a couple of friends thinking this way things can come together very quickly and you'll find yourself enjoying some more fun and less stress sooner. It's good for everybody. Give your friends the gift of longer life, more fun, and better looks by giving them their own copy of my book. Improve friends' lives and help pay for my daughters' braces at the same time.

The exercises and games I teach later in this book are easy to learn and will get you on the right track. You'll learn from this book and other sources, but you'll really *get it* when you play, so get the message to your family or friends who will play.

It's true that some types get it more easily than others. Sometimes getting it has to do with career training and sometimes it's personality, but it can be pretty hard to tell which of those things lead. Some professions that historically get the improvisation message and run with it are educators, entrepreneurs, caregivers, managers/supervisors/team leaders, groups going through change or forming a new team, and young people; those folks get it quicker.

The main advantage the young grown-ups have in improvisation, other than physical resilience and flexibility (sigh), is that they probably remember more play than their older counterparts. Middle-aged grown-ups have more references and more experiences to draw upon, so their improv can have more interesting dimensions. Still, sometimes the middle-aged ones can be almost tragically serious.

Kids, of course, get it like crazy. One of the most fun things I get to do is work with school-age kids in improv outreach programs. They get it almost instantly and run with it and many of them never forget what they learned. I bump into them as grown-ups and they still have the look of play in their eyes. The only troubling thing I see in my work with kids is the evidence that for many of them play seems to be a secret language that lots of the people in their lives don't speak. They are thrilled to see someone who speaks play and you can see their souls light up when an adult knows that language. We can and will all help each other on this eventually.

We need more people out there with play skills and we will hit a critical mass where we don't put up with stuffy crap and rudeness and uninspired work. We can do it. We all need it and so it spreads when encouraged. We love it and recognize it when we see it like we recognize the light in a child's eyes or a fun pup or a smart reference or a big grin from a good friend. My family gets along better because of it and yours will, too.

Once you've had a good time improvising you might find renewed interest in other engaging and fun activities that you had let slip away in your life. Improvisation and play are exponentially good in that way. They'll make other things you do a lot more fun. Your time with others will seem better. What is really happening is that you are feeling better about yourself and others and are more interested in life. And being more interested makes you more interesting.

Where to Start?

Start with this book and the exercises and games in it. Once you know the basics you might want to find a workshop so you can be with like-minded people and a capable teacher. There you can experience variety, group mind, ensemble, and a place to play in a non-judgmental environment.

If you need professional training services you'll need one of the few great pros; but for a beginner's workshop for individuals, there are lots of choices. You might have a good beginner's workshop opportunity right where you live.

There are highly recommendable "franchise" operations to choose from. For beginners and amateurs I'm particularly fond of National Comedy Theatre, ComedySportz, Theatresports, IO, and Second City organizations. There are outstanding independents, too, some of which include one or more of the franchise relationships listed above. These include SAK Theater, The Groundlings, Upright Citizens Brigade, ComedyCity, and many others. You would probably find these in the theatrical listings of your local paper, or certainly with a search on the Web. If the groups do performances, you might go see a show and decide if they look like a fun group to learn from. Some charge more than others for workshops or events, but it isn't a very expensive endeavor.

Here are some specific recommendations. Austin, Manhattan, San Diego, Los Angeles, and San Jose all have National Comedy Theater operations with great training schools. Some of these also have ComedySportz franchises. Kansas City and Green Bay have good training schools with ComedyCity. San Francisco has Bay Area Theatresports. Milwaukee is the home of ComedySportz and has a great program. Chicago is loaded with improv training options. There are many more, but these are all very good. Also look for quality programs in Richmond, Raleigh, San Antonio, Boston, and most other U.S. cities with populations in excess of 250K or with a college community. You can also check your local community college. You can even take a class while on vacation in Amsterdam, at some Club Med resorts, or on some cruise ships. There are many options for those who want them. And they all speak English.

If you do a Web search you'll find plenty of schools. Improv groups were quick to move into cyberspace and you'll find a bunch of stuff if you look. Choose thoughtfully; and go with the most experienced or a reference from a friend if you can. Check 'em out first with a free taster class or something relatively cheap and see a show. Most are inexpensive, but like anything else, cheaper is not necessarily better. *Yesand. com* is a popular improv site to reference and there are many others.

Start at the beginning with an entry-level workshop. Many improv organizations offer tasters, or a free first class, or a chance to audit a class for an hour or so. Try to get a class with fewer than 15 participants. I prefer 12. The teacher should be nice and fun so meet them if you can, perhaps at a show. If you like your classmates maybe you'll want to progress to the next level together.

You can expect a 6, 8, or 12-week series, depending on the organization. Often they are called levels, as in, level 1, level 2, etc. Your class fee may also include admissions to one or more shows. Advanced levels probably come with performance opportunities for invited guests. It's important to perform. It cements what you have learned. Even if you don't intend to perform in your life, you should do a little workshop show for the experience. You'll never forget it and you'll have a great party story.

CHAPTER 12

IMPROV BASICS

It's kind of fun to do the impossible. — Walt Disney

A great improvisation is both impossible and natural. It goes like it is supposed to go. It went exactly like it should have. It's amazing how many "keeper" pieces of work come out of improvisation. This is partially because you are allowed to go where *things lead you*. For instance, when I was in the TV business briefly I got a TV show picked up. It was an improvisation show. When the network executives had said that they were nervous about improvised TV, I replied that their scripts were usually riskier than improv. With improvisation bad paths get dropped and great ones get followed, it flows like water, gracefully circumventing obstacles and making it to the pool in short time. If you launch into a script and find it is bad or inappropriate, good luck. You are stuck with that script for another 40 minutes. Ow! We sold the show when the networks recognized the truth in that.

Games and Scenes

Most improvisation work consists of practicing and using exercises, games, scenes, and eventually extended structures that blend these things together. There are dozens and dozens of games. There are many longer, larger structures, too. The list is endless and growing. It is a wide-open and creative field.

Anyone can learn games. Most of our favorite improvisation performances are games. Games and exercises overlap. Some do well on a stage and some are more fun in the practice room or your living room. Games are durable and fun and can hold character and parody choices which is always fun. Exercises get you in shape for playing and are totally fun in and of themselves. It is pretty easy to get good at games. Everyone loves the games. I've known about 100 players who were hands-down GREAT in games and they were players who had mastered most of the improv disciplines and could do about anything. I think that games are great. Love 'em.

Anyone can do basic, even strong scene work, too. Scene work is based on a few core values, but ultimately it is a more refined skill than games. Scenes can have literary aspects. They are mainly about relationships, setting, and additive choices, but they can also play with arcs, subplots, allegory, twists, chapters, all sorts of devices. But we're mainly going to talk about games, short scenes, and scene games. They are the most fun and if you love them you will naturally move into other stuff. Let's look at some basic elements of games. We'll touch on the essential *Yes and* and delve into relationships, setting, and IFHE. Oh, and failure. Don't worry; you'll get it.

Yes, and...

Since the most important takeaway for all of us is the message of *Yes and* we will now look at it for the second time.

The basic concept that drives improvisational creativity amongst players is usually called *Yes and*. The idea is that an idea or inference is offered and the other player agrees with it by adding something to it. This is beyond acceptance; it is additive. This is the basic fuel that makes improv go so fast and travel far. This way the outcome is often just as surprising to the players as it is to the viewer. Also, the outcomes are usually more interesting than if one person had driven the moments instead of *Yes anding*, which is how improvisers describe using *Yes and.*

Yes and extends into how you choose to lead your life. It doesn't free you from the need to judge your commitments, but it certainly does free you from being harmfully judgmental. Some of the most exciting sequences of your life will come from saying, "Yes, and." This is a far-reaching truth, friends. Mark my words! This is a guarantee. If you learn the power of the *Yes and* it will change you and present you with bounty. Often life is offering you a path and you are not accepting it. You'll need to consider the truth of this.

"IF YOU LEARN THE POWER OF THE 'YES AND' IT WILL CHANGE YOU AND PRESENT YOU WITH BOUNTY."

Relationships

One thing common with virtually all improv methodologies is that relationships within the improvisation matter a lot. If there aren't relationships in a scene or a game it can be difficult to get interest or traction. Imagine no relationships in your life, or in your favorite books. Relationships give everything substance that fuels all the other choices in life and in art. For instance, one person explaining how to file taxes might be dull, but an H&R Block worker explaining next year's tax code to his dying rich aunt might be interesting. Or a pre-teen explaining tax codes to his dad might be fun. The relationship is at least as important as the idea and they empower each other.

Who What and Where

Another thing we like to do in improv is play with the elements of setting. Stories without a setting suck. Sometimes an element of setting can really make a scene go. I remember a fun scene where two party buddies are in their car rocking out and talking about all the wildest rock concerts they'd been to.

Kinda funny characters, environment, and relationships. But the scene really landed when we found out that the party buddies were cops on duty in the Dunkin Donuts parking lot.

When in doubt, an experienced improviser might tell you, "Go to the where." That means strengthen the sense of where you are by doing something to help show environment and strengthen that context. Like relationship, the setting elements of who, what, where, and when can give you the context for very fun and interesting play.

Failure

In the real world, failure is treated like a real thing, an absolute bottom. Some people would say that failure is a sad, tragic thing evocative of pity. In actuality, that description of failure is human paranoia run amok! Failure is no such thing. Failure is an attempt that didn't go exactly as intended or didn't function as well as one wanted. If there were no failure, there'd also be no development. Failure that comes from a bold attempt is celebrated in improv. It is fun, funny, and admirable. It is a jump off the high dive and a sure sign of progress.

> 'FAILURE THAT COMES FROM A BOLD ATTEMPT IS CELEBRATED IN IMPROV. IT IS FUN, FUNNY, AND ADMIRABLE. IT IS A JUMP OFF THE HIGH DIVE AND A SURE SIGN OF PROGRESS.'

Think of Edison and the light bulb. He claims to have failed at creating a light bulb about a thousand times. Aren't we glad he didn't take failure tragically?

Think of finding a path in the dark. Occasionally you would step off the path, and, in so doing, you'd determine where the path was. The failures along the way were the reason you could succeed.

So always try your best and go for it and if it is a failed attempt, have fun and try again and congratulations, we're all proud of you for going for it. By ignoring the man-made false idol of failure you give it your best, time and time again without any burden. It is a track to fulfillment not judgment. Failure is likely to define your path to success.

IFHE

Another way to describe the whole improv process was propagated by improvisational legend Del Close. Del was an inspiration to an entire generation of improvisers. He is most identified with The Committee and Second City, but he affected most of us who were around during the early years of the improv boom.

It might get described a little differently from place to place since so many companies use it, but here is how I learned it: IFHE, as in Initiate, Further, Heighten, Explore. A variation is AFHE: Agree, Further, Heighten, Explore. Same deal really. This is a great way to look at the process and in no way conflicts with any of the other ways we've already laid things out.

A player initiates a scene with a line or an action. This is the first line or action of the game or scene. It is received in the spirit of *Yes and,* perhaps literally with those words. For instance, Player One *initiates,* "I didn't know it'd be so tough to make it as a lawyer on a desert island. I mean, it's kind of lonely." The second player furthers the idea with "Yes, and that's why I took correspondence courses to pass the Bar exam, Bob. I've become a lawyer, too." In so doing, Player Two *furthered* the elements of the initiation, in this case with a literal, "Yes, and."

Let's say that soon there is another development where Player One says, "Two lawyers could have a lot of lawsuits. Shame we don't have people who want to sue each other. (They look at each other hungrily.) Unless…." Setting up the realization that they could create endless lawsuits against each other would be a *heightening* of the risk and general stakes in the scene. Another way I describe this, is that we pulled this scene from a longer story because it was the important one. We as the improvisers who are creating the scene have to discover why the scene is important. We have to find what heightens it to a vital level in the larger story.

Having initiated, furthered, and heightened the scene, now the improvisers are free to enjoy *exploring* what they've built. They can launch frivolous lawsuits, make accusations, parody the legal system, cannibalism, whatever their interests and play choices lead them to.

IFHE is a fine recipe for improv work. It is totally compatible with the other values we teach in this book. You'll find that you'll eventually have more than one way to think about your improv. You might think about what is most fun, or what is most additive with *Yes and* or relationship and setting, or you might see the process best through with IFHE. It's all good.

CHAPTER 13

IMPROV FOR FUN AND HEALTH

Da dum, da dum, da da da da dum… — Don Johnson

I t's important to jump into these exercises and see how they work. Sometimes you may not understand them fully, but if you do the exercise or game whole-heartedly it will some-times reveal great things to you.

Beginners and newcomers are exciting to watch. Even though they sometimes struggle, they have flashes that can be bril-liant. The quote above is from a man named Don Johnson. Not the actor, no, but a smart and kind fellow in Austin. He took workshops with my company and even made it into the main stage company for some time.

Don had graduated from our workshop training and was per-forming in a workshop show. The workshoppers were closing with a game called ***World's Worst.** In *World's Worst*, a topic is taken from the audience. It might be a celebration or other event where people get together—a wedding, for example. All the players line up across the back of the stage. Players step forward when inspired, taking turns offering the worst thing that might be seen or heard at a wedding. It gets a laugh or it doesn't. The player steps back into line and another takes the center spot with a new idea on the same theme. When there is a pause in ideas the host changes the topic. The players try to keep the center spot hot and keep things moving.

Anyway, the suggestion Don's workshop group had was "funeral." Don steps forward solemnly. He is standing before a casket. He looks down to the foot of the coffin and sees a crank sticking out of it. He grabs the crank and slowly starts turning it. It plays music while he stares at it curiously. It goes, "Da dum, da dum, da da da da dum…" (Pop Goes the Weasel – the tune from all Jack in the Boxes). The crowd, and yours truly, laughed their butts off.

Private Play

Let's start with some fun private play. Private play can be like a wonderful secret that gives us a lot of energy. For instance, an excellent actor I worked with from the Royal Shakespeare Company used to sneak off before a comedy show and make funny noises to himself. He'd try to make himself laugh. Every time he recalled it that evening, and even when not consciously thinking about it, he'd feel the energy of that playfulness wriggling inside him. He'd have access to a five-year-old's energy for the evening and all from a minute or so of playing funny noises in private.

Private play is also a way to build and maintain other play skills. Gibberish is a great play tool in various ways for every discipline we're discussing. Driving to a show I often put on a Spanish or any other non-English language radio program I can find and attempt to parallel it in gibberish. Use the inflections, sell the Coke, warn about the weather, enjoy the variety of tones and sounds. It can be tricky but very fun. And private. It's a great way to get ready to learn to communicate with, yes, gibberish. Knowing good gibberish opens up other great possibilities that we'll get to a little later.

Another great one for the car is listening to Pop hit format radio and making up lyrics to songs. Start simple, don't try to

make up all of it, just have a funny chorus that sounds something like the original and see if other stuff comes to you. Then
sing it loud and proud and have fun in private. Music gives
flow and makes you feel good and responsive to life. That feeling of responsiveness is needed for a lot of things.

Some other private play I indulge in is humor-based stress
management. There are many funny tricks for stress management. Dick Chudnow, founding father of ComedySportz, gave
me this next idea. It is especially powerful for a high stress
event or day. He suggests taking a small slip of paper, couple
of inches long and half an inch wide or smaller. On this paper
write a funny word you
love. I have a friend who
uses the word "Chic-o-
stick" for his funny word.
This piece of paper gets
hidden in your underwear.
It'll change your attitude
because you have a little
play secret. This can
give you a hint of smirk
and humor that is your
little secret and keeps you
energized.

"DON'T FEEL LIKE A
DORK, GOOD READER.
YOU'RE GONNA GET
QUICKER SMARTER
FASTER MORE PRO-
DUCTIVE INTERESTED INTER-
ESTING BETTER-LOOKING
AND LIVE LONGER WHILE
HAVING MORE FUN."

Playing privately is great and will always be good for you, but
you need to learn to play with other players.

Feel Like a Dork?

Don't feel like a Dork, Good Reader. You're gonna get quicker
smarter faster more productive interested interesting better-
looking and live longer while having more fun. Right? So? What
Dork? BUT you might feel like a Dork the first time you suggest
an improv game to your friends, right? I can help with that.

First of all, many great improv games and exercises come
from two fun realms of our shared experiences. What I mean
to say is this: we have taken the best games from the peri-

ods of life you liked the most. First, we have some kid games. There are some very pure and forever fun kid's games that we played really well as kids. Later in life many of us played those games again in college, but with alcohol added to the process. Seems we have fits of enjoyable play transitioning into grown-uphood. Perhaps some dark panic slips up on us as we realize that somebody may expect us to stop playing once we cross the event horizon. We need to shake that bleak paradigm.

Anyway, using this to your advantage you could try playing with kids first. Six to ten-year olds are pretty good to play a simple game. Or try a playful grown-up friend. I love to play little improv games with my children and my wife. But you could introduce a game as a great party drinking game if you wanted to and you'd be telling the truth all the same.

Here are some fun ideas that might seem attractive to you once you are playing. You could have a game night and include an improv game. In so doing you are creating a time for play that can get you closer to these goals. Making music is a great way to build these types of strengths and relationships, but everyone doesn't play instruments. (They should!) Sports are a good way to build some of these principles and bonds as well, but everyone doesn't like, or just can't play, sports. Play how you want to.

Many healthy activities can bolster your ability to Play Well With Others but none get as close to home as improvisation. Improvisation uses interaction, communication, thoughtfulness, and surprising fun in ways that these other methods don't. It'll make you feel more like you. The good you.

Play Well With Others

Some exercises and games are best played with a certain number of people. Let's start with two-player warm-ups, games, and exercises, of which there are not many. Here are a few of my favorites. Whether you use these as a warm-up, game, or exercise is up to you and depends on how much fun you have with it or think you can with it and with your particular partner. I've used most of these on and off stage.

*Alternate clapping** is good to get physically warm and focused for play. Two people face each other and one claps, then the other claps, repeat. They go on clapping alternately. The goal is to get evenly spaced claps and speed it up until it sounds like applause. Over 15 seconds or so you can start and go faster and faster until it breaks. Try again and improve on it.

Issues that might come up in *alternate clapping* are that you could hurt your hands. There is no prize for hitting yourself the hardest. Take it easy and go fast not hard.

*Trust walk** is a great exercise that builds mutual trust and confidence and a sense of taking care of your play partner. Player One closes their eyes tightly. If they find this uncomfortable or they open their eyes uncontrollably, then a blindfold is  "PERHAPS SOME DARK PANIC SLIPS UP ON US AS WE REALIZE THAT SOMEBODY MAY EXPECT US TO STOP PLAYING ONCE WE CROSS THE EVENT HORIZON." OK to use. Player Two leads them verbally on a walk. Player Two can explain, "Walk forward towards my voice. Stop. Take a small step to your left. Now forward again." Etc. Take the blinded partner on a walk and experience doorways, halls, different qualities of light and sound indoors and outdoors. After a few minutes, trade roles and walk back.

Issues that might come up with the *trust walk* are ones of safety. EXTREME CARE must be taken. The player with their eyes closed is showing great trust because this exercise does instill fear, if even on a supposedly light level. They can't be allowed to touch or bump anything. This is very serious. Trust can be damaged instead of improved if great care isn't taken. When you get really good at the exercise you can experiment and do it impromptu sometimes.

Options with the *trust walk* include **trust walk in a circle** where the player can walk freely with their eyes closed while their fellow players gently catch them and take care of them, gently directing them back into the center area. This is best done in silence.

For the wildly adventurous there is also **trust run.** *Trust run* can be done with the player sprinting 20 yards or less with two great physical players ready to catch them. The running player holds their arms out to the sides and down so that the catchers have a great way to catch them.

For an amazingly adventurous application of this exercise you can try the **open field trust run.** This is one of my all time favorite things to do. Player One has their eyes closed or blindfolded and runs freely on a smooth field of grass. Player Two can yell necessary instructions to them to keep them safe. Occasionally I'll do this solo on the beach or somewhere where I can judge my position and avoid obstacles for brief periods of blind running.

*Things in... is a warm-up game where one player asks another to name five things in a category. For instance, name five things in Einstein's sock drawer or name five things in Angelina Jolie's purse. The other player gets to use their imagination to answer. This comes in handy later in performance games because you are ready to go when you list items or contents. This can also be played with friends all at the same time, and, yes, Party Reader, it can even be another drinking game, if you must. Let's say there are five of us in the living room. One of us names the title, such as five things in Mother Teresa's backpack. Then each person in the room must name an item. When it is complete, all take a swig or a shot or slap themselves or whatever you think is fun, and then right back into the next round taking turns.

Issues that might come up with this game include excessive wackiness. Explore the balance of normal and truthful to odd or absurd. It'll have more texture and fun if it is plausible as well as wild. You can use friends and personal references, too, like five things in Bob's closet.

Here are some good games and exercises for three to six players.

*Zig Zag Zor is the warm-up that I have used the longest. It works best with four to eight people, but it's flexible. It is known alternately as Zip Zap Zop, Zig Zag Zorg, Bud Wise Er, Z cubed, etc. Players stand in a small circle. Player One looks clearly at another player and says, "Zig!" The player who received the zig looks clearly at any player and says, "Zag!" The player who received the zag looks clearly at any player and says, "Zor!" When "Zor!" is said, the person saying it simultaneously claps. The player who receives the zor looks at any player and says, "Zig!" Etc. So, it will sound like "Zig! Zag! Zor! (clapping at same time) Zig! Zag! Zor (clapping at same time) Zig! Zag! Zor! faster and faster. The game continues as fast as the players can maintain it, until someone makes a mistake.

Some mistakes are hesitating when you should have gone, saying the wrong pass at the wrong time, not clapping on the Zor, clapping after the Zor instead of on it, anything that breaks the speedy flow of the waltz beat that is this game. It's good to call mistakes quickly and firmly, celebrate and get right back into it.

My favorite way to deal with a mistake in *Zig Zag Zor* is for everyone to celebrate by putting their hands on the shoulders of the person left and right of them and pushing their crotches all to the middle of the circle saying, "Aahwoooga!" Then go at it again, faster and clearer and see how far it can get. It's great to go as fast as you can, ride it, then celebrate the mistake and dive right back in.

If you have a large group, sometimes it is fun to eliminate people when they mess up and see who is triumphant as the last person standing. If you do eliminations, it is important to do it more than once. You will probably learn that different people win at different times. This truth helps to make the eliminations not feel like failures.

Variations on *Zig Zag Zor* can be played separately or simultaneously. Basically, instead of passing Zig Zag Zor, you pass

Bud Wise Er, Hi Neck Ken, Zip Zap Zop, or another trio of your choosing. If played simultaneously, then the rule is that you must finish whichever one is launched and whoever's turn it is as a new trio of passes is launched can choose the next trio of words. For instance, after "Zor," the next player could pass "Bud," and the next two would have to say Wise and Er, or they'd have made a mistake. With **Zig cubed**, the first player passes Zig and the second player also passes Zig, and each pass must be used three times until the trio of passes has gone by, then the choice is open again to go Zig Zag Zor or Bud Wise Er or whatever is chosen. The level up from this is to allow any pass that can be caught in threes, always keeping the clap on the third pass. I call this **Wide Open Zig Zag Zor.** For instance, "Butcher!" might yield you "Baker" and "Candlestick Maker." "Stop!" might get you "Drop" and "Roll." If it works, it works and you keep speeding along. If someone launches one that can't be caught then they made the mistake.

*Gibberish conversations are always fun. The skills this game develops will help with a lot of different things, too many to explain at this stage of the process. To start with, just have fun with it and see if you can let it flow. It is an important exercise and has lots of performance and training applications as well.

Pick a style of gibberish. You can choose a style of gibberish either by paralleling a real language that you don't know and drawing from all the best-related references you can think of. Or you can choose a batch of sounds, a character choice, a sing-song tone; it's wide open. You and your partner attempt to speak the same language, devising it jointly by listening to each other well enough to use and reuse words that each other has used in the conversation. That lets it build specificity and credibility and get more interesting. It also is a challenge to find the strengths and weaknesses of your particular gibberish menu. It builds on how well the listener listens and the reaction time that allows the things said to be heard as important things. The more real the reactions, the more succinct the vocabulary, the better the conversations.

Issues that might come up in *gibberish conversations* include one player deciding the other is crazy, or worse, disagreeing with them angrily. What the heck? It's gibberish. It's kind of a personal choice to decide to get angry and combative. It is better for everyone if you use *Yes and* and occasionally allow yourself to be quite fulfilled or changed by what the other is saying. Choose for it to be a great conversation.

*What are you doing? is a great gamey game that is mainly identified with the ComedySportz show. It is an excellent game amongst friends. Two players stand. Player One starts doing something active through mime, like pretending they are riding a bike. Player Two asks the question, "What are you doing?" The question isn't asked coyly or with character; it is fired at the player punctually. Player One must then answer with something active that has nothing at all to do with the activity they are doing. They might say, "Walking the dog." Then Player Two starts miming that activity, walking the dog. Then it's Player One's turn to fire the question, "What are you doing?" Player Two answers with something that has nothing to do with walking the dog. Perhaps they say, "Brushing the president's teeth." Immediately, Player One begins miming brushing the president's teeth.

This goes on as fast and as creatively as the players can go until one of them is eliminated for repeating something that was already said in the game, or hesitating, or saying something that in any way resembles what they were actively miming. When a player makes one of these mistakes they are eliminated and a different player gets a chance.

One variation is to let one player manage the game. The player/ host will start the game, make any necessary calls (they are *always* right), change and obtain themes, etc. Players can rotate through, even the host player, so that everyone gets a chance. We often call this, "King of the Hill" style.

Issues with *What are you doing?* include trying to start with a verb when answering. The beginner will want to say, "I'm," which gets redundant and is kind of a stalling tactic, too. It's better to start with a good verb like running, scrubbing, melting, etc. Another issue is making it too wacky, too early. It is good to start it simply and speed up and let it get wilder as it develops.

Options with *What are you doing?* include taking topics or themes for a round. Ideas might include a popular movie or book, or perhaps a place or a hobby. Then all the comments must somehow satisfy the topic or theme, thereby raising the level of challenge for the players. The truth is that some players play better with themes, so you should give it a try. You can also do this with initials. When doing that, you start every comment with a "B" like bowling, boxing, etc. You can even take an initial, two initials (one each for each of the first two words) or take an initial *and* a theme and they have to do both at the same time.

* Don't panic, but you have an Enlarged Appendix. In it you'll find a section entitled "Plays Well With Others - The Games" where this game and the others in this chapter can be referenced.

IMPROVISATION FOR BUSINESS

*There cannot be a crisis next week. My schedule
is already full.* — Henry Kissinger

All businesses benefit from the skills that improvisation and play bring to their team. Productivity, adaptability, agility, ethics, enjoyment, turnover, healthcare, and the elusive but powerful team spirit are some issues businesses can improve with improv. In this chapter, we'll overview some Improvisation for Business basics. There are exercises and games within each topic.

Listening

*I like to listen. I have learned a great deal listening carefully.
Most people never listen.* — Ernest Hemingway

Listening well and maintaining our listening skills are of utmost importance for a successful and enjoyable business interaction. The power of good listening has many benefits. Most of us suffer to some degree with an inability to listen. This skill needs regular training and maintenance. I've trained business groups extensively on this. Often it is the single largest gap in their processes.

Most of us listen to someone until we think we get the point and then much of our attention wanders into formulating our response or figuring what we are going to do after work or who knows what else. We need to learn the skill of listening to someone all the way to the end. To not do so is neglecting a very valuable asset. It is sooo valuable. One of the stresses of business organizations is not having enough information. Listening helps you get more information. Another stress in business is unaccountable employees. Listening helps with making people accountable. Listening also helps with respect, productivity, and a host of other issues.

One of the best questions I was ever asked by a business leader while training on this topic was, "But what if the person you are listening to is just saying a bunch of stupid crap?" Nice, huh? My response was, "You are surely right. If you have decided that it is stupid crap, then you won't get anything out of it, and, therefore, it is stupid crap."

This supervisor had a choice to listen well or not. Consider this from the perspective of the employee reporting to that supervisor. If your supervisor doesn't listen well, then you are free to say just about any dumb stuff you want. If she isn't listening well, you probably won't feel accountable or follow-through with your ideas anyway. So the supervisor's bad listening skills create the exact situation she is trying to avoid.

When you listen really well, you instill responsibility in the speaker. She gets the impression that something is expected from her and that she has value. Also it gives notice that this will be remembered, there will be responsibility, progress, follow-through.

Try this exercise called ***First Letter Last Letter.** Players stand or sit in pairs. Player One starts a conversation about anything they wish, for instance, "I sure like watching NBA games." Player Two responds to the conversation, but starts with a word that begins with the last letter used by Player One. In this case, Player Two might say, "Sure. Me, too." Now Player One will respond with a word starting with the letter

O. Maybe, "Other sports stop too much, but basketball is quicker." This goes back and forth for a couple of minutes.

Are you listening all the way to the end? Listening to the texture and detail? Could you retell it well? Can you hear the speaker having to be more responsible for what and how he is delivering to you? Your improved listening keeps speakers on their toes and more accountable. How did it feel to listen all the way through? Could you tell that you don't always do that?

After listening well, *show* them that you heard by your actions. Do something in the direction the conversation took you. They'll get the new scenario quickly, you'll see.

I'm sure you'll find life richer and communication stronger if you put these practices into place. In a short while you'll start to see less miscommunication and better reporting. You'll be able to reclaim some of the energy that you've had to spend in re-communicating and patching over botched jobs. You can instead put that energy into follow-through and support, easing your burden in general.

Improved listening will help your staff work better and be happier in their work. They'll begin to feel more recognized and respected. And all you did was listen better. Pretty cool, huh?

> *A good listener is not only popular everywhere, but after a while he knows something.* — Wilson Mizner

Communication

I like to think of communication as a game of catch, as passing. My favorite way to start on this is by playing some simple ***Ball Toss.**

When was the last time you tossed a ball around? I suggest you play some ball with associates. Take a tennis ball, a small, inflated ball, and a beach ball and pass them back and forth in a big circle of 10-20 people. You can pass by tossing the ball across the circle anywhere. Emphasize safety and soft throws. Emphasize that some balls will get dropped and that's no big deal.

"SOME OF YOU CAN BARELY MANAGE TO KEEP A SMIRK OFF YOUR FACE AS WE'RE TALKING ABOUT BALLS; ADMIT IT!"

Notice how people use eye contact, timing, types of tosses, etc. Notice how people react to dropped balls. Do they just pick them up and put them back in play? Maybe some people hold onto balls and don't pass them at all. Some of you can barely manage to keep a smirk off your face as we're talking about balls; admit it!

These ball games have a real clarity when it comes to passing, don't they? It's always interesting to me that when we play games there's no mystery about who is keeping the ball cleanly in play. One thing that all the best passes have in common is an early beginning and a strong finish. This is very different than just "getting the ball off," or just "getting something off of your desk." In a gaming sense, we might describe the process in these six steps…

1. Have a good grip on the ball yourself. If you don't have the pass thoroughly in hand, you probably won't pass it well. In a communication this would be, *understanding what you're going to pass before you try to pass it*. A key to this is listening well.

2. Decide what and to whom you're going to pass. This is another part where you had better listen and observe well.

3. Make it clear whom you are going to pass to by giving him an unmistakable indicator: a clear look into the eyes, calling her by name, checking on the receiver's readiness. There's listening in this part, too. You must be aware of the other player's situation to pass in a way that will succeed.

4. Pass in a way that's good for the catcher. Make a pass that can be caught. Remind yourself that if it can't be caught, it's your mistake and you still have responsibility for the ball.

5. Stay with your pass to see that it was caught and carried. Hitting hands doesn't mean it was caught. The indicator you're looking for is the catcher's ability to advance the ball.

6. Follow-through. Every great athlete speaks of follow-through. Help your pass to succeed. That might mean support of the catcher, clearer intent, or repeating the pass.

Our work and lives will be less stressful and more productive if we support our teammates with quality passes. Bad passes encourage your teammates to be irresponsible about catching and carrying the ball. Good passes and follow-through make everyone more responsible and productive without having to put in more effort.

Your assignment is to try this process and observe the results. It is a very satisfying thing to toss balls with coworkers. Options to spice this game up include using patterns. For instance, pass a ball around until everyone has had it once and no one has had it twice. Then pass it again. Can you recreate the pattern? Let it go around the pattern multiple times and keep it going. Now try putting extra soft balls of various sizes and shapes in the pattern at the same time. Now try putting the beach ball in the reverse of the pattern. Now try creating a new, additional pattern of words from a category (types of food, sports items, etc.) and do the ball patterns and word patterns at the same time. Maybe start by trying two tennis balls in one pattern and two softballs in a different one at the same time. It's good to do something strong enough and difficult enough to engage all of your attention. That creates focus and allows you to clearly see the reflection of your communication skills in the *Ball Toss*.

Business Decisions

In any moment of decision, the best thing you can do is the right thing. The worst thing you can do is nothing.

— Theodore Roosevelt

Business decision-making tends to come in two primary flavors. There are readiness-based decisions, where we have the time to decide, test, be sure, sleep on it, request a study, whatever we can do to make the best decision. Most of us prefer these types of decisions. There is security, whether real or perceived, in this type of decision-making. We also spread the blame pretty thoroughly. But if you could, you would probably choose this type of deciding process.

"IN IMPROV, WE SOMETIMES SAY, 'MAKE A DECISION. THEN MAKE IT THE RIGHT DECISION.'"

Then there's timeliness-based decisions, where the decision must be made now, not later. There are lots of timely decisions demanded of us. Surprise developments, emergencies, opportunities, crises, these occurrences and more create narrow windows for timely decisions. Timely decisions can have a success rate as high as ready decisions if the skill is developed. In general, some of the time and energy that couldn't be spent getting ready gets applied in the follow-through and support of the decision. In improv, we sometimes say, "Make a decision. Then make it the right decision."

A great game for this is *Expert Definitions. Player One gives the other a gibberish word. Player Two then confidently gives the definition to that new word, citing its roots or origin or whatever else shows their expert knowledge on the subject. Every answer is correct. Then Player Two gets to offer a word to Player One for definition. It can also be done taking turns in small groups. The point of the exercise is to practice stepping forward confidently when asked, stating the answer and figuring the rest out as you go, supporting the assumption with evidence that comes to mind during the decision. Everybody needs the ability to depend on what they've learned, and their instincts, and going for it. Everyone needs to feel like an expert once in a while. Everyone also needs to be reminded how strong and fast their minds are in the moment if they will commit to starting immediately.

Co-creativity, Collaboration, and Teamwork

These issues are different but related. In my upcoming book on "Improvisation for Business," I go into much depth on the strengths and differences amongst these concepts. For now, I've included a taste of each training track to get you thinking and learning.

For a good co-creativity exercise, go to the appendix of this book and find the exercise called *Two Eyes on Paper. I've provided a worksheet so you can try this exercise, but you'll see that you can create your own full-size pages easily. Basically there is a blank sheet with two dots where eyes might be if you were drawing a face to fill the page.

I usually pass around a box of crayons and let everyone choose one each. Chalk on a chalkboard or pens on paper work OK, but do not use anything too faint like pencils or lighter-colored crayons. Players form pairs and sit together. They'll need a flat surface to make it easy to draw on the Two Eyes sheet. Be silent for the duration of the exercise. Player One makes a single mark on the page, perhaps an eyebrow over an eye. Player Two then adds a mark. Taking turns, they draw a face. This continues until there is a significant pause whereupon the players should consider if the drawing is finished. Once finished, Player One puts a letter at the bottom of the page. The next player adds a letter and they take turns until a name is formed. The name might be gibberish or a traditional title. Then players should share and comment on how it felt to lead or follow, the concepts of variable leadership, how neither is responsible but both are, etc. Sometimes you learn a lot on the second run. Be sure not to let the length of the exercise grow. It only takes a minute or so to do a picture once you settle into the process. The tone of the room while this happens is light and laughter erupts from time to time. It's very refreshing for a team to be in an environment of lightness and laughter.

Collaboration in business is usually more about productivity. How can the two of us, or the 10 of us, combine our efforts for optimal output and ease? Without collaboration skills, a team gets exhausted and members stop liking each other. With collaboration skills, there is often amazing output with no additional effort.

A great starter exercise for collaboration is the *****Yes and** Party Planners.** Two players face each other. Player One suggests they throw a party for their team. Player Two responds literally with, "Yes, and," adding whatever he chooses. The players take turns *Yes anding* the other player's suggestions and encouraging whatever direction and flow the thing takes. Let it develop to its most flagrant degree without forgetting the initial reason for the party. The plan may begin as an employee appreciation day and end as a concert in Hawaii; there are no limits, but it must build through *Yes and* responses. It's important to enjoy the other player's ideas. This exercise usually takes less than a minute. Once the skill is learned it has great applications. You could try it with more players and nurture additive commentary on your team. You can load it with real and specific subject matter instead of a party. You could launch brainstorming sessions with it. You can do it in a brief break time to exercise the skill and have a laugh; it takes maybe 30 seconds once you have a handle on it.

Lastly, teamwork is a by-product of nearly everything we do. There are many teamwork exercises in my work. *****Dance Diamond** is adventurous and is often the closer exercise at my workshops. (I usually don't say the name because it scares people to talk about dancing in public.) You have four people stand in an open area. They stand about six or eight feet apart, as if at the points of a diamond. They all face the same direction, so three of them can see the one at the front clearly. The one at the front is called the Point Player. Music is played. I choose music that makes people move, but doesn't cause them to think too much. I've been known to use Motown (just about anything by the Funk Brothers), James Brown, Ray Charles, and the Beatles. Anyway, the Point Player is directed to create some movements, dance if they want to (everyone dances, but some like to pretend they are just moving about). The three players seeing the Point Player from behind must copy the movement in unison with the Point Player. When the Point Player turns 90 degrees, a new Point Player is created and they seamlessly continue with the new Point Player choosing their own movements. The three behind them now match the new movements. This continues. The Point Player can walk and crossover other teams of four and still maintain their process.

Issues that come up with *Dance Diamond* include objection to even doing the exercise (though most will remember it as the coolest thing they ever did), leadership, agreement, variable leadership, following, engagement, etc. Is the Point Player doing moves that are fun but can be followed? Or is he doing abrupt things that don't show an understanding of being followed and matched? Can the individuals express themselves clearly and unselfconsciously? It isn't an exaggeration to say that *Dance Diamond* has changed people forever right before my eyes. It makes a number of things clear and it definitely demonstrates active learning with flow. It blows some people away because it is so simple. I have created *Dance Diamond* addicts from the Bahamas to Hawaii, Canada to Mexico. I love it every time.

Other Good Exercises and Games for Business

A fun game for marketers, advertising pros, manufacturers, product industries, and brain-stormers of all types is ***Slogans**. Slogans* is played with two to 20 people. The game starts with a real product, say milk, or a specific brand of something like Krispy Kreme or Tide. Then the group starts throwing out ideas for the slogans that were *rejected* for the product. It can really allow the players to blow off steam and only takes a moment to energize everybody's attitudes again.

Exercise your creativity. There might be one idea offered or five, but as soon as there's a significant pause, take another product real fast and keep the tempo up.

Another really short but effective game is *Wrong Name. In *Wrong Name*, a team or an individual takes a minute to choose things around the room, point at them, and firmly call them something that they in no way are. For instance, you might point at a chair and firmly call it, "Pudding!" But what if you called that chair, "Dog?" Perhaps you know that you called it a dog because you were thinking of its four legs. That would not be doing the exercise because it uses logic. The goal of this exercise is to shake you out of logic's death grip, the one that develops because you stare at projects too long. Of course we rely on our logic, but if we can't escape it then we get to where we don't see the logic forest because of the logic trees. We must be able to shake off the shackles so we can go at a problem again freely, so *Wrong Name* is a great short way to exercise that, even when alone. But do it with your team for 30 seconds before a meeting and enjoy a better meeting.

*Things in Common are important for building inroads to community on a business team. Here is an exercise of that same name. At a gathering have people talk in pairs for two minutes, then in different pairs for two minutes. Direct them to find interesting things in common. Uninteresting things would include, "We work at the same place. We both like movies." Mundane stuff like that doesn't help. But, "We were both cheerleaders in the eighth grade. We both love the movie *Casablanca*. We both bass fish competitively. We both traveled in remote Asia when we were 20 years old." These things change the way you see each other and create reinforcements in the fiber of your community at work. For some industries, this is huge. I just taught it to a big fundraising branch of a major university in regards to developing relationships. It also worked well with a major hotelier.

Issues that come up with this exercise involve the different ways interesting things in common come up in conversation. You have to listen closely and open to different pathways. Information can be dug out purposefully by asking questions or you can offer things up. Perhaps the best way to find things in common is through having texture in your conversations, staying present, and encouraging quality communication. People with interesting things in common have stronger communications and can't go backward. Great communication deepens the context of relationships. It never ceases to amaze and surprise me what coworkers discover in common in this short exercise. Incredible things. I've seen cousins find each other for the first time. People shared an ex. Won the same award as a kid. Both secretly give all their free time to feeding the hungry. All kinds of stuff comes up when you are willing to share.

'PEOPLE WITH INTERESTING THINGS IN COMMON HAVE STRONGER COMMUNICATIONS AND CAN'T GO BACKWARD.'

Other Skills

I've developed entire "Improvisation for Business" programs to develop networking skills, presentation skills, and other necessary business skills. The issues of credibility and authenticity and the ways that play and improvisation support those concepts comes up a lot. These topics are beyond the intended scope of this book, however; so I'll save those for the "Improvisation for Business" book I plan to release soon. Luckily, if you apply yourself to the exercises we already discussed in this chapter, some of the benefits will rub off on other areas of your work and life, including those I just mentioned.

* These games, like that chewing gum you swallowed as a kid, can be found in your Enlarged Appendix. They are in a section entitled "Plays Well With Others - The Games" where this game and the others in this chapter can be referenced.

CHAPTER 15

IMPROVISATION FOR PROFESSIONAL ENTERTAINMENT

There are some things you can't share without ending up liking each other. — J.K. Rowling

Hello, cousins! We recognize each other and are relieved to see each other. If you are just now becoming a professional, then welcome! You'll find positive and generous improvisers all over the world if you approach them as a positive, generous improviser yourself. Congratulations. It's a fine network to be in. I have many associates who I share with. I give jobs away and have jobs given to me all the time. These are valuable relationships that I enjoy for life, hardy associations based in extreme fun, business ambition, and the arts all at once.

What do I mean by "professional entertainment?" I would describe pro entertainment as working responsibly in the market and having a refined skill set at not only performing, but at managing clients and events. There are a lot of skilled improvisers who aren't professional. That is, they do not make all or part of their living as improvisers. Professional improvisers make all or some of their income from improvising. Fortunate folk, they are.

As a player/producer, I see improvisers develop in cycles. It usually goes the same general way. We find a talented player. We train them and play with them intensely for a few months and get them settled into the basics and into the ensemble. We wait until their playing has fun and freedom to it and they know enough improv games or structures to get through a show. Then they do some shows. If they are doing OK, you keep expanding their menu of games and get them through maybe 20 to 50 of the easiest shows available.

At some point their show skills come together pretty thoroughly on their home stage. More often than not they have a year of shows behind them by then. I know many players who are *excellent* in their home theater, but the majority of them can't go out of their theater for shows yet. There is a vast gulf of experience between the player/producers who can travel and do remote shows and those who are only good on their home turf.

Players who excel in their own space, but don't get out much, often obsess on the quality of what they are doing. A pro, on the other hand, tends to put more credibility in the quality of the audience/clients' experience. For instance, a subtle but sure sign of a pro is how they accept a compliment after a show. I have to train newer players on this constantly. When an audience member says, "Thanks! That was great! Hilarious!" You smile and say, "Thanks." You can add a little something like, "Tell your friends" or "See you next year" or whatever, or compliment their town, but basically you smile and say, "Thanks."

Excellent amateurs find this challenging. They are already giving themselves and their fellow players notes in their minds. When told, "Thanks! That was great!" all they want to say is, "The musical usually goes better than that; you should see us when Tom is playing," or something apologetic. They don't realize that they are insulting the audience experience. It's almost like you are saying that they are dumb for liking a sub-par show. It's a terrible thing to do to a nice person who just wanted to share their excitement for your work.

Pros give and take some notes after every show but that has nothing to do with respect for the audience experience. A pro is likely to feel that any show that the audience loved was a great show, regardless of the professional development notes that they discuss amongst themselves in private.

Tech Skills

You have to master the tech skills necessary in your theater. Are you heard well? Seen well? Are you heard and seen evenly throughout the room? Can your music be loud and clear? Many groups perform in intimate spaces where they are less subject to these issues. As your show grows, you'll need to make sure that you keep standards high for these basic tech needs.

If you want to get good at travel shows or simply take bookings, then the player needs to learn other stages and situations. Similarly to how you got them into shows, you should get them onto other stages. One development opportunity is getting into a festival where you can share stages and workshops. Maybe you can get a chance to do a show for a group in a nice theater with a good tech staff and you soak up everything you can learn. The great road-show player/producer knows so much about the various aspects of the show.

In addition to knowing staging, lighting, travel planning, communications (phone system, e-mail, a plan), you'll need to know microphones (which to use and how to use them). Sound, lighting, and staging are the basic elements, and these are the wrong places to skimp and save. You want great sound especially. Does the show you have planned work best with area mics or lavalieres? Mics, choir mics, shotguns? Will you use a wireless handheld or two? Did you use simple SM58s with cables where you could? For big shows I usually have a combination of these items for different purposes. The room, the sound system, and your show are key elements for making tech decisions. Sometimes decisions are influenced by client preconceptions, event coordinator rules, who knows what else.

I'm good, but not the best at everything every time. Another sign of being a pro is recognizing when you can or should hire the better producer. I've done it for groups and I've had producers do it for me. For instance, I am very good at sound, floor plan, working the lighting, staging. But if a room is too big or tricky, or if the stakes are really high (guest stars, dignitaries, cameras, lots of money being spent, huge audiences, etc.), then I hire a top producer. I have a producing friend and associate named David Perkoff who can set a room for sound like nobody's business. He is certainly one of the best producers for big events, but he keeps the names of two or more engineers handy for when he needs to have a better pro in that position.

Never forget *The Mystery Problem*.

Management

To become an improv manager, you'll need major management skills. Even if you have a manager, there's no escaping the need for your own heavy-duty management skills at the professional level. Managing a group in this situation takes skill. Managing coworkers takes skill. Managing clients takes a very long list of skills. Your players usually don't know everything you know and that has to be OK. Your clients might not know what they are doing and that has to be OK. That's why you are there, so don't get frustrated with them. Instead, quietly take care of them beyond their surface requests, but in the way they want and need. Make your fellow players and your clients look good.

'MANAGING A GROUP IN THIS SITUATION TAKES SKILL. MANAGING COWORKERS TAKES SKILL. MANAGING CLIENTS TAKES A VERY LONG LIST OF SKILLS.'

You might have to make relative and compensating decisions without showing any stress. Always remember that you are the pro and they may or may not know anything about producing shows, so you are often responsible for the success of the event, and that is not limited to the performance content by any means.

Event Design

Even the best clients and gigs have design flaws. Sometimes I get hired to work out the design and flow of the entire event and sometimes I have to overview it and help the client even though I wasn't hired to do so. It's a bottom-line approach to the event. I can't have my success in the hands of someone with vastly less experience, but it takes skill and savvy to get some events quietly into shape beforehand.

A great place in the lineup or flow of events can make every-thing else go better. A bad design or flow can make an event un-win-able. Your client may or may not know the difference. This job could have been assigned to your client by his boss. Who knows? Most of my clients are pros at what they do and give me great designs or challenges; *but* even the great ones deserve your collaborative overview. Go through it in your mind and see the flow, and look for potential obstacles and opportunities.

In many spaces you don't have choices about ground plan, but in many you do. It's the same with sound and lighting. You have to research it and see what it needs. Try to interface directly with the tech person. Know their name and get per-sonal. You usually can believe what they say, because they have done it before, but be careful and think it through.

I'll tell you some general things to avoid, but this is a frequent realm of *The Mystery Problem*, so think it through every time. Some of these things you can control and some you can't.

Don't let them separate you from your audience. Beware in big banquet halls and roadhouses. Some theaters even have orchestra pits or dance floors that separate you from the audi-ence. That never helps. You want to be up close where the audience can see your expressions, hear your natural voice, feel that you are all in an intimate space. You also don't want the audience itself to be too spread out. Use the smallest seating arrangement or room configuration that will accommodate everyone well. In many theaters we play in front of the arch or even in front of the curtain, it depends on lighting and sound, and any et ceteras.

Don't let them serve dinner while you are onstage. Don't let them put you too late in the event or schedule you for too great a length of time late in the event. Don't let them put you or your audience in inhospitable sun and heat. Don't let them bill you concurrent with other events, unless they advertise or spread the word some efficient way. Even if you work clean, don't let them call it a "kid" event or in some cases even a "family" show.

I go into this stuff much more thoroughly in my upcoming book for professional improvisers. It includes sample contracts, invoices, types of deals you cut for various types of gigs, marketing, and the related hard-to-come-by information.

For now...

Let's Talk Improvisation!

Different groups have different strengths at different times. Some groups wail on replays, or musical games, or maybe they rock at active scenes. You need to enjoy the strengths of that team and not miss the opportunity to work on an excellent skill set. When I'm on tour with the National Comedy Theatre Manhattan guys, they rock at guessing and replay games. When I'm in Los Angeles, the National Comedy Theatre/ ComedySportz guys rock at styles. The Chicago improvisers tend to love creative and wild structures of scenes and tag-outs, subplots, stuff like that. Each of those groups offers a different set of opportunities to further myself in those skill sets and I take them.

Some of My Favorite
Pro Warm-Ups and Exercises

To get to the top of your craft in this industry, you will have done so many exercises and shows that your warm-ups will naturally adapt and develop over time. Before I go to a show, I do some warm-ups for myself, like I stretch briefly, check my vocal and diction state of affairs and maybe do a few exercises, if needed. Sometimes I do a character or two or sing along with the radio if I'm driving to the show. The main idea is to get to the group warm-ups already set to go.

In our group, we do a little of what we want, maybe stretch, count, sing, do some quick reaction stuff, whatever we feel like. Though the warm-up games come and go, cycle in and out, there are consistencies. We often do about 20 minutes together before the show. We fill it with exercises, chat about what we feel like playing in the show, chat about the needs of the particular room or audience.

Before a show I love to play *One Touch. *One Touch* can be played with some sheets of newspaper wadded up and wrapped in clear tape. That makes it kind of a ball about 8 to 10 inches in diameter. A beach ball is OK, but too slow. A roll of socks makes a pretty good ball, too. The goal is to keep the ball in the air and in play without anyone catching it and without the same player touching it twice in a row. In a circle, a player tosses the ball up. Another player gets to hit it one time, like with her open hand, usually, and then another player hits it. It's like tapping it into the air. There's no predictable sequence; players just operate instinctively getting out of the way, covering for each other, whatever it takes. See how long you can keep it up.

When warming up with a great group, I usually want it to include a kid game or a silly song we do together. That way we do something musical and something in unison, and nobody is too darn cool. We're more fun.

Good warm-ups are replete with physical activity that is even sillier. A great sing along I enjoy is "Wishy-Washy Washer

Woman." "Tootie Ta" is pretty darn good, too. I can't teach you those tunes in the book, but you can ask a kid. Or go ask a kid for a good silly song in the first place. They might offer you "Aye Guzumba," "Crock Dilly Oom Bop," "Mary Mack," or who knows what.

*Kitty Wants a Corner is a great kid's game. It is one of my favorite games to start a practice session with. It's especially good in groups of 10 or more. Players stand in a circle. One player is in the center. That player is "It." *It* walks up to a player in the circle and says, "Kitty wants a corner." The player in the circle replies with, 'Go ask my neighbor" and *It* walks to someone else and makes the same statement, "Kitty wants a corner." This continues. While this is happening other players try to make eye contact and sprint to trade positions before *It* can jump into one of their vacated spaces in the circle. While players dart back and forth trading places, eventually *It* gets into one of their vacated spots and now the new stranded player is "It" and play rapidly continues.

Take a look at the first instructional section where I described *Trust Runs.* A good practiced group can do some very adventurous trust work and I recommend it. Definitely try some *trust runs.*

*10 Characters is an excellent practice activity for your group. One player takes the stage and goes into a character. When the character is established a bit, in say three to eight seconds, the director can yell, "Switch!" and the player on stage goes into a different character. This goes on for 10 characters in a row. Fellow players should support the character changes with appropriate responses. *10 Characters* should take a minute or a minute and a half at the most.

Discuss where the character choices came from. It would be really hard to go rehearse 10, so how did you get 10? Consider that some came from physical choices, some from psychological choices, some from our past, or from archetypes or careers. Furthermore, the player learns about their resourcefulness and how well they can commit to choices on the fly.

If your group focus is feeling scattered, few things work as well as *Counting Together. Counting can be done more than one way, but start like this. The group sits in a circle quietly. Someone says, "One." Someone says, "Two." The goal is to count comfortably up to 20 or more without any two players speaking at the same time. No patterns. Just whatever it is, it is, and did the group find its balance and ability to count up past 20? If it takes a few tries, which it often does, try counting down from 20 instead - it sometimes freshens the exercise.

Recognize that everyone should be in. Nobody should be in too damn much. Pattern-lovers often think if the same person always goes first or something the game will work, but that rarely helps anything. It is partially about listening, not just to sound either. Equilibrium of contribution makes itself clear when counting this way.

Music, Style, and Movement

Here are a couple of my favorite games to do with professional improvisers. You gotta do some musical games and full-blown musicals. It is just too challenging, too rewarding, and too good for the group to pass up. Not just musicals, but musical games, too. Watch some musicals, or bands, or rappers, or parody something on the radio and get warmed up to the idea. A singing coach might make for a few fun rehearsals. Find a like-minded, rockin' musician. Usually you want a piano player, especially one who masters preprogrammed beats. I've seen a few guitar players do well at this, too. I've also had great fun with accordion players, trumpet players, and a trombone. Remember when shopping for a musician, there are mainly two types of music. I like the good kind.

You should also play style games. Let's look at *Shakespeare first. Shakespeare uses lovable plot devices like long-separated twins, disguises, ghosts who explain stuff, flowery language; it's totally ripe for creativity and parody. You need some people in your group who are knowledgeable about the style, but if a couple of folks aren't, it can make for a good mix, too.

Watch a movie of a Shakespeare play. Even better, you can go see a show together as a group. Basically, you will try to use all the devices while working on a scene suggestion. It is parody and homage all at once. Consider going into the house and not being bound by the stage for some of it. Enjoy some stock characters like a gravedigger, a fool, the King, the maiden, the Knight.

If you can get the hang of *Shakespeare*, you can potentially do any style. Try **opera, film styles, film directors, TV shows**, the sky is the limit once you get the hang of parodying styles.

For movement, go to the Enlarged Appendix and look up *Dance Diamond* in the "Games" section and use it to put choreography in your musical improv. It is an amazing trick. Not only can you make improvised movement amongst teammates look like rehearsed choreography, but the concepts at play in *Dance Diamond* will affect other skills positively. It's not only for dancing. Let the concepts sneak into your other movement decisions. You can match physical choices of other players or match movement during the tasks and activities your team creates. Pretend to be kitchen co-workers or on a construction site. Almost all settings can benefit from some amount of application of movement skills.

And did I mention…

Yes, and…

Since the most important takeaway for all of us is the message of *Yes and* we will now look at it a third time. This is at least as important for veterans as it is for beginners.

The basic concept that drives improvisational creativity amongst players is usually called *Yes and*. The idea is that an idea or inference is offered and the other player agrees with it by adding something to it. This is beyond acceptance; it is additive. This is the basic fuel that makes improv go so fast and travel so far at times. To not accept and use ideas would be blocking. This way the outcome is often just as surprising to the players as it is to the viewer. Also, the outcomes are usually more interesting than if one person had driven the moments instead of *Yes anding*, which is how improvisers describe using *Yes and*.

Yes and extends into how you choose to lead your life. It doesn't free you from the need to judge your commitments, but it certainly does free you from being judgmental. Some of the most exciting sequences of your life will come from saying, "Yes, and." This is a far-reaching truth, friends. Mark my words! This is a guarantee. If you learn the power of the *Yes and* it will change you and present you with bounty.

"WHEN I MEET THE MYSTERY PROBLEM I SAY, "OH, SO IT'S YOU?" THEN I SOLVE IT AS BEST AS IT CAN BE SOLVED."

If you put down this book having learned nothing else, at least remember the power of *Yes and* and you will have gotten some real value.

Start a Group and Book a Show

I suggest you gather some funny friends who improvise, have some auditions, get a little gig, and give it a shot. You'll feel great, even if it isn't your career path. Consider a gig at a restaurant/bar happy hour, or a short set of games at an open mic night. Invite friends and family and see how much fun you can have. You'll never forget it.

The Mystery Problem Returns!

Don't forget to allow for it. When I meet *The Mystery Problem* I say, "Oh, so it's you?" Then I solve it as best as it can be solved. I might also have an emergency back-up Shure SM58 in my briefcase anyway, and a different colored shirt in case the backdrop or lighting was *The Mystery Problem*. I also request an additional mic ready by the stage. And I know the sound guy's name. I'm just sayin'…

Be smart and expect *The Mystery Problem* and solve it. Sometimes you have to change a lot over the darn *Mystery Problem*. In those instances, turn it into a strength that makes for a rockin' show. In that way you still kick *The Mystery Problem's* butt and you still get to have fun.

* The Enlarged Appendix is in the rear. Of this book I mean. There you'll find a section entitled "Plays Well With Others - The Games" where this game and the others in this chapter can be referenced.

CODA

COMMUNION
COMMUNITY
COMMUNICATION

*Man is most nearly himself when he achieves the
seriousness of a child at play.* — Heraclitus

Whether you are playing for fun and health, business success, or to learn to perform professionally in improv, the basic values remain the same. The simple aspects of imagination, listening, additive agreement, relationship, heightening, and play are the main ingredients in your toolkit. You can learn more complicated concepts, but these simpler ones never diminish in importance.

Play cannot help you if you don't play. Reading this book probably helped, but you won't know the real benefits of play unless you actively play. Improv play has natural mechanisms to build your confidence and reward your collaboration, so it will calm your nerves about those things as you do it. Let the improvisation and play get into you and you'll never regret it.

We have the power to know success and to love our community and that power is fueled by the principles of play and improvisation. I know the things I have told you in this book by experiencing them time and time again in the crucible of humanity. They are real and tangible. These concepts, and all other concepts, live and breathe in the moment.

In the moment, you are sitting at the crossroads of everything. You are at the confluence of not only everything you ever learned, thought, and intended, but also at the center point of where you are going and at the hub of all your opportunities. Anything that keeps part of you out of the moment diminishes your opportunities in the moment. That is to say, preconception and concern for outcome hamstring your potentialities in the moment.

Love the moment and feel the advantage of having to make decisions in the moment. There is no more powerful place if you know it. All you have learned and all you can be meet in that moment.

You improvise constantly. Embrace it and play with it and get more out of your life and work. Watch it reflect back on you in your work, your team, and your family. You'll feel more like you than you've felt in a long while.

And play. Play Well With Others. It's the highest skill on your grown-up report card. Watch your troubles dissolve as you play. Notice how your successes increase and how much better you feel about them. Feel your blood surge as you play and laugh. Feel friendships deepen as you beam into each other's faces, bursting with laughs and creativity.

You can increase love and feel excitement, camaraderie, creativity, quickness, and energy. It can be your normal state if you nurture it and let it grow. Even a little of this play and humor will change your outlook and your relationships. There's no maybe about it. If you apply yourself to it, you will find many of these truths waiting for you.

My parting words to you are to use the games in this book and go play. Then follow your instincts. Support your teams and enjoy the benefits in fun and productivity and success. Play with your family and watch those relationships flourish. Watch your own attitudes and skills flourish.

Together we can make the world a better place, both subjectively and objectively. We can be part of the waves that wash the world with positivism, ethics, and human value. Things should be fun and brilliant in this world. We have the perfection of all. That is what we have to thank for the way improvisation and play works in this world. If we are in the game, then things go exactly as they should. Enjoy life by living happily on its currents and enjoying the extreme bounty available to us in the moment, the amazing wealth that becomes available to humans who have strength of community. Give yourself the time to see the brilliant solutions, the power of group mind, and the staggering strength of poise in the moment. And, above all, the power of *Yes and.*

"PLAY WELL WITH OTHERS. IT'S THE HIGHEST SKILL ON YOUR GROWN-UP REPORT CARD."

ENLARGED APPENDIX

AN IMPROVISED LIFE ON THE ROAD
Tour Journal Excerpts

FIVE BASIC RULES FOR IMPROV SCENES
Compiled by Tyler Bryce

PLAYS WELL WITH OTHERS: THE GAMES
Quick Reference Guide to the Games in This Book

IN THEIR OWN WORDS
The Power of Improv and Play as told by Artistic Directors, Veteran Players, and Clients of Improv

AN IMPROVISED LIFE ON THE ROAD

Tour Journal Excerpts

Here's a description of a tour: we flew to Germany, got on a bus, and drove around doing shows for a few weeks.

You could describe a tour that way. On the other hand, the same tour could be described like this:

We had a life-changing set of experiences with 18 shows in 21 days in three countries. We saw castles and rivers, mountains and forests, and learned an intensive lesson on humanity through the citizens and the soldiers. We honed our craft and turned in some great shows, even though every single setup was unique and had significant challenges for all the different reasons a show can be challenging—from managing ourselves on the move to different sound systems to bad sightlines to language barriers. It was epic.

Both of the above descriptions are true. The lesson is the same as the lesson of life. If you allow life to become flat and meaningless, it is a choice. If you choose to see life in living color, teeming with past, present, and future, with lessons and beauty pouring out of it every step of the way, then that is a choice, too. I certainly choose the latter.

These are some journal excerpts from two overseas tours I did with National Comedy Theatre that were produced and managed by Gary Kramer and Kimberly Chase of NCT in NYC and San Diego. I want to share the beauty, oddness, and surprise I encountered. Touring is one of the most improvised ways of life I have ever known, even more so than vacationing. It's totally hard work, but it's great. Touring like this uses all your skills, and as a pro that feels great, too. You'll see my geo-awareness decline from cities and dates to the simple descriptive, "next day," due in large part, to the wondrous disorientation of being thrust into new worlds day after day.

The first tour started in Egypt and went to Crete, Greece, Italy, Corsica/Sardinia, then Spain: 18 shows. The second tour was in Germany and the Benelux circuit, which is Belgium, Netherlands, and Luxembourg. For that one we played 15 shows in theaters, clubs, amphitheaters, tents, auditoriums, and a big gym. We got print, radio, and TV coverage throughout. We played for multinational companies, U.S. military and their families, embassy staff, and all kinds of local and non-local audience members. It was a life-enriching set of experiences, which is exactly what Gary told me it would be when he got me to take the first tour.

It was 24 hours travel time to Cairo. I meet the two younger players on the tour, Justin and Pete, and we start to check each other out. The producers and I have drinks and catch up. Sleep, wake up, and sleep again. By the time we arrived we were daffy beat. Our first accommodation was to be a cushy hotel downtown where we'd be for three days and two shows. We emerged from the airport to a minibus and an armed guard. Surprise! You're headed into the Sinai by the Gaza strip. Thus we started...

The Tour of De Nile

As it gets dark we are speeding through the desert with our headlights off. All the drivers had their headlights off. If yours are on, they flash at you like you are crazy dangerous. We stop at a roadside place to use the bathroom and have a beverage. There's a big picture of Osama bin Laden behind the cashier. We push on through the dark, nervous and tired. We get to a UN checkpoint and they don't like our equipment and bus. Turns out they are Columbians and I get to speaking Spanish with them and explain. Our handler gets us through and we are into three days in the Sinai.

Day 3, Sinai, Egypt

I'm now writing from the southern tip of the Sinai Peninsula on the Red Sea, which is a LOVELY body of water. We did a show last night in North Camp Sinai, a MFO camp (multinational forces and observers) about eight miles from the Gaza strip on the Mediterranean. Last night I actually felt an explosion from a distance as I was told I might. A lieutenant was going to give us a helicopter tour and show us the Gaza and Israel from the helicopter over the Med, but some event changed that. We drove to south Sinai today; seven hours along the Israeli border, many checkpoints run by Fijians and Colombians and then the U.S. Many 18-year old Egyptians with Uzis and such. The Egyptian soldiers at checkpoints, we have learned, get virtually no bullets and are for show. We can see Saudi Arabia and Jordan from this camp. I should mention that even though we have worried a bit, we are being kept very safe, I think, and the scariest miles are already behind us. Tomorrow we're on a long ride to Cairo (unless we can sneak a helicopter ride) and we do a few shows from there. We might get to visit Giza and the Sphinx and Pyramids the morning after tomorrow. Yeah! The Sinai, and Egypt for that matter, are very desolate, yet full of civilization; in the Sinai that civilization is mainly nomadic Bedouins and they are amazing, but I have no time to describe them. Desert, huts, goats, and cell phones.

Day 6, Beni Suef, Egypt

I am in Beni Suef, Egypt, about halfway down the country on the Nile in an agricultural oasis on an Egyptian air base entertaining the personnel here from the U.S. and other western countries. Had a really fun show. The team is totally settling into the run now. Justin and Pete are great kids, really talented. Pete and I in particular are quite a pair and having a blast with it. Gary and I always have good shows and fun. We are getting it on now!

Before driving out of Cairo, we saw the Pyramids, and, oh my, they are impressive. Made it into a tomb, a pyramid, and a sphinx. There are over 30 pyramids and multiple sphinxes, obelisks, etc. Giza was fascinating, got a great photo of it including one from the Pizza Hut /KFC across the street.

Outside Beni Suef our driver and embassy escort decide to ignore a checkpoint, which is scary. We pass a large painting of Al Zawahri, the Al Qaeda leader, and it is surrounded with flowers in an area where they should barely grow.

The tour is going great. Some fun and no incidents to speak of. We are gearing for another all-nighter of travel to Athens and then Crete for more shows. Egypt and Sinai have been very interesting. I met many people including many Texans and Austinites. Won't miss Cairo or Egypt THAT much though— it's a little...challenging.

Day 7, Cairo

I'm playing pool at midnight right now in an embassy safe house surrounded by armed guards in Cairo, about to leave to catch an overnight plane to Athens. I just really wanted to say that, since I can barely believe it. We performed outdoors at the Cairo American Embassy tonight. Turned in a very good show. Pretty cool tour so far. Much of my effort is in managing myself with the travel.

Day 8, Athens Greece

We left from Cairo airport in a grueling series of events at 3am. Pete and I got into a delirious laughing fit about something and laughed until we cried, until we passed out for a while. In Athens, we convinced the international clerks at the airport to let us leave and return during our layover and took 90 mph cabs (a recurring trend in Greece) to the Parthenon, Acropolis, Theatre of Dionysus, Temples of Zeus, Athena, and much more. Appreciation has been extremely high, since Egypt and the Sinai lowered/raised our awareness of comfort so much.

Off to Crete, home of the Minoan Culture, seat of civilization, birthplace of the bathroom. What a lovely place. What a lovely lifestyle. What a lovely waterfront on the Aegean Sea. We swam. You can see as far underwater in the Aegean without goggles as you can in a swimming pool, although to say both in the same sentence feels crude.

The Greek meals began. Oh, my. Start around 8:30 or 9pm, get maybe 10-12 plates on the table of creamy cheeses, yogurts, salads, local barrel wine (each town and region has its own, sometimes each establishment). Then dinner would come. Usually a mixed grill of meats, including a half dozen each of pork chops, lamb chops, beefsteaks, sausages (country style, kinda dry and very tasty) chicken, unfreakin' believable. They come afterwards with fruit and raki, an incredibly strong liquor done as a shot, or for me two, after dinner, very chilled. Only in Crete. There has been live music at EVERY meal. Usually outdoors. The entire process of dinner tends to wrap up about 11pm. Families are still out, since everyone takes siesta or reposa each day.

We are playing better and better and Crete was our first overwhelming response en masse. Standing ovation and they don't let us leave. Sweet soldiers from home need to talk and we oblige, though I've learned to nurse drinks to try to keep up. More cab rides on little country roads at 80-90 mph, no lanes, and, usually, no headlights. Took a quick spin by one of the local monasteries and back in time for our flight to Larissa, Greece.

This time we flew ASCOMED, which is a military flight, and it kicked ass. A 10-seater that pulls up to our building and drops us off at our next base: no transport, no airports, nothing. Nice Navy pilots and crew who took us into the cockpit and asked could they chauffer us around Italy a bit. YES! We played cards in the back in facing seats with tables as we watch many of the 2,000 Greek isles speed by. Had a near collision experience with F-16s, but we are in such good hands I never sweated. F-16s! We were at a base of them in Crete. I say just, show a couple of those and a couple of our professional soldiers to any potential bad guys and see if they still feel like fighting. Ridiculously impressive. To see a series of them go shooting up in short runs and short successions at night, rocket blast shooting 30 feet out the back in bright white with blue vertical lines interspersed, maybe five jets in one minute... shooie!

Next day...

So we land in Larissa, Greece in the famous Plains of Thessaly. Like Crete, the countryside is almost nonstop elderly olive trees and vineyards. We speed past Angia Pouli to our show straight away. This time we had some kids and families and it was a NATO base. Another standing ovation and here comes Perry, the self-titled "coon-ass" of the base, with shots of the local beverage. My third coast cousin has brought us an amazing beverage. It is Tsiperou, which is Ouzo's meaner, yet wiser, older brother. We're all laughing drunk and are pretending to drink the beers that came with the little shots that could. ONE shot each and we're giggling wide-eyed with numb, hairy tongues. The coon-ass is confused why we don't want more. Justin is pie-eyed delirious. My pal Pete walks with a bottle. Off to Angia Pouli for another three-hour Greek meal. The town square has filled for a concert from the local music school. Children everywhere, old people walking with hands behind their back flipping their little Greek orthodox prayer beads placidly in their hands. Seven-year olds watch after their younger brothers and sisters while older kids chat. Parents sit with beverages and argue politics. A toothless old man gives me some kind of gelatinous almond dessert called Holva and says, "Texas? Hey, Clinton! Cowboy!" It's explained to me that they don't get a lot of visitors here in the Plains of Thessaly. We're military flying to Sigonella base in a couple of hours for another show tonight. We'll be in Sicily, and then we'll go on to mainland Italy.

Next day...

Yeah, you know how your eyes feel drunk after looking at art for a couple of hours? My mind body eyes and heart feel that way. My freakin' concepts feel drunk even. I'm off to a beach in Sicily and then tonight our show is sold out at a 400-seat hall. The three seas I've been to so far are the Red Sea, the Aegean Sea, and I'll soon visit the Mediterranean Sea. Yesterday I flew over the Adriatic Sea in a small plane.

Next day...

The show last night in Sicily went great, an exemplary show with lots of play. Then we went to dinner from about 10:30 to 1 and had seven types of seafood, two types of pasta, two types of water, two types of wine, another round of fish, and sorbet. Unbelievable. At the fish market in a wonderful cushy six-table restaurant where you don't order, they just start. The best olive salad I ever had. Stinkiest street in the civilized world. Got approached by an "Umbrella Girl," a sad prostitute from a foreign land managed by the local organized crime. They are brought into the street life under the false pretense of paying off a "life debt" to obtain their citizenship. They are used until deported. Ridiculously sad state of affairs.

Here's a true piece of dialogue with a Sicilian associate yesterday. He was wearing a watch and I wasn't.

Les: What time is it?

Sicilian: I'll tell you.

Les: When?

Sicilian: In a few minutes. Relax.

Next day...

We perform tonight in Naples and tomorrow in Gaeta. Today we get to visit Pompeii. I can see Mt. Vesuvius and I think of my Mom every time I see it.

Next day...

We stopped in Mondragone on our way to Gaeta and had the best sandwich I've ever had in my life from this little store. We ate them on the bus. They were full of Italian meats, veggies, bufalo mozzarella, olive oil, spices, and all on focaccia. They were so good, we were on the verge of tears and brainstorming on how to save some, but it was temporal and we loved it.

Next day...

So I'm in La Madalena. We flew into Olbia and drove and ferried to La Mad. Yesterday we started our only time off (day and a half) and we got drunk on Corsican beer and Grappa and swam naked in the clearest most hospitable sea I've ever seen. Laying on big flat, moon rocks. La Mad is a very small island between Sardinia and Corsica in the Med west of Italy and south of France (it's Italian). We're in a nice hotel; I'm bunking with the fun young bachelors, and we have a view from our terrace of the sea and other islands in a breathtaking panorama. We are not in sacrifice mode at the moment, but instead managing our health and rejuvenating for a grueling five-show, 5,000+ mile closer that often includes overnight flights and same day shows. To some of you, drunken swimming might not sound like rejuvenation, but you know...today is swim, gym, eat, nap, repeat.

Next day...

Mama, I had insalata di mare, pizza Napolitana, and penne arrabiata for dinner last night and thought about you. We walk around on this little island and every sight is wonderful. Mom, you would especially like the cute little blue and white boats. Chris, you'd love it all.

We'll perform for the fleet here tomorrow, then, Katy, bar the door for a week. This is our third naval installation and the sailors are quite different from the soldiers. We don't talk politics, but they sure have been.

Next day and through the end of the tour...

I last wrote after a glorious first of almost two days off in La Madalena, Italy. We had a great show in La Madalena and were very sad to leave, sneaking in as much last minute swimming, kayaking, biking, and EATING as we could. It was a naval station that is one of four nuclear sub support bases in the world. Little theater in a rough building, no AC, but very appreciative audience. Homesick families. I got very comfortable speaking

Italian, which is funny because I only seem to remember it (or even know it) when surrounded by Italians (thanks, Mom).

On the trip from the Olbia airport in Sardinia to the ferry for La Madalena, we went through some mountains. Part way through a mountain pass the back door of our transport vehicle sprung open and suitcases, PA, mics, and all sorts of stuff went scattering and skidding about the road. Very little damage, all in all, but my suitcase, which I bought a few hours before leaving Texas, will be retired due to that and other damages when I return. I think we have taken 16 flights, about as many van trips, and we still have two or three flights left. About halfway through the trip, I lost track of the itinerary—you know, after it changed once or twice. I would just ask what time to be ready, what country or city was next; each leg of the trip became a joyous surprise.

The archipelago (the La Madalena area) between Sardinia and Corsica was just great. Water visibility like a swimming pool. It's so salty that no one drowns because you float so well. Happy goats, happy dogs, happy boats, happy food, and happy Italians.

We were allowed to sleep three hours our last night there. From La Madalena (3am, post show dinner lasted until midnight like usual), we bounced out of Rome airport yet again (9am) and off to Pisa (noon). Great base in a huge grove of those southern European pines that are all trunk with a huge canopy at the top like an umbrella or a mushroom. Pine cones that will knock you out if they land on your head. We did laundry glamorously and ate crappy base food, took a nap and did a show same day. Show rocked. Set an attendance record for the base. Lonely, hardworking, overextended soldiers this time. Wanted to talk all night and we had no stamina left, but ate ballpark nachos with them, nursed beers, and did our best to socialize.

Our host took us to old Pisa in the morning and we saw the leaning tower, Duomo, Basilica, and rain. We have gotten giddy for lack of sleep and too much comedy and took pictures of other tourists for our 90 minutes there. We were in Pisa slightly less than 24 hours.

Straight to airport for a flight to Madrid then to Rota, Spain; Andalusia, I think. Rota is a big naval and air force base in a town of 30K, about an hour north of Gibraltar on the Atlantic side of Spain, south of Portugal, a couple of hours north of Morocco.

Lovely place with cobblestone streets that are walled, hiding the courtyards of homes within. Walking and scooter-only streets. The best paella I've ever had. Families everywhere all night (Saturday night). Even near midnight there were families sitting at bars around the plazas, bouncy inflated games for the children in the middle of the square. Lots of old people. Had a few moments of extreme anti-American sentiments thrown our way. (Not the first time or first place, I just haven't wanted to write about it.) Spanish is my second language and it was often useless here. The dialect is close to Castilian, but the vocabulary includes much Italian and no Mexican. We got to swim in the Atlantic on Sunday morning and grab some quick tapas before our Sunday matinee, which had families and rocked. More lonely Texans gobbling up my stories of Texas afterwards.

We get to sleep until 4am tonight! Then off to Madrid tomorrow (Monday) and another show same day (matinee that the base is giving an afternoon off for). Then we have Madrid for an evening.

We got the day to visit the king's castle and some of the beautiful sights of Madrid. We got the evening in Madrid, and, oh, my. Me and the boys blew off some steam! We sang karaoke in a little hovel of a grilled mushroom and sangria bar. Had tapas in a bullfighter bar. Hung out in Plaza Mayor. Walked all through downtown. Our host took us to a handful of bars in walking streets somewhere in downtown.

Tuesday morning I'm off to Madrid airport for my flights to Atlanta and then home to my beautiful three girls, wonderful friends, roots music, and enchiladas. I believe I arrive a couple of hours after I leave because of the time difference.

Sad to say goodbye to the team. What a great team and tour. They are my siblings forever.

A few months later, Gary, Kim, and I and my old artistic director Tyler got to do a big show out of NYC. What a blast. Six months later Gary calls me for another tour. Amongst other things, I am booked for a big original theatre piece in Austin called "Keepin' it Weird." It is getting press on the national news, *Wall Street Journal*, and the covers of all the local arts publications. All my various producers and friends conspire to make it work for me and I am off for a tour in Europe. So starts...

The Lords of the Rhine

Day 1, Germany/Benelux

We make it to Frankfurt and get our 15 pieces of equipment including PA, piano, etc. The Germans are looking awkward and expressively fashionable, lots of small face hair like half moustaches, multiple thin lines on cheek, and many men with lines of hair down the middle of their chin in a soul patch/goatee/skinny line of hair. Up walks our new friend and bus driver, Sylvio.

We had worried about the bus. We spent much of last tour on planes and vans. This tour is lots of bus with only two flights—one in and one out. If the bus is good, it'll be a breeze. If it's a glorified van, it could suck with six people and 15 pieces of equipment. We are hoping against hope that it has a bathroom.

The bus. Halle-freakin-lujah. We got the tour bus. The big red lobster. A full size bus. All the stuff goes under it nicely in big bus hatch doors. Bimbamboom, easy load. That's important because it's a highly repeated task for us. A bad ride for a tour like this is like a bad pair of shoes on a marathon. With a cute little hiss, a mid-bus door opens and slides sideways like a spaceship door, or the door of the contraption in *The Fly*, and I go up the stairs. Holy crap, we got the good ride. Couches, table/booths, four little bunk sleepers with privacy curtains and windows, a mini kitchen and a nice bathroom we'll only use when we need to be good to Sylvio, and, omigod, an espresso machine. I quickly make it to the back area of couches, flat screen TV, DVD player with case of DVDs, fridge of Beck's beer. We are deliriously happy zombies now. The autobahn goes flying by as we play with everything like giddy kids. Deliriously happy zombie children. Chris and Dorian immediately start *Braveheart*. The surreality, aided by exhaustion and intermittent sleep, is kicking in good.

Gary and Kim are co-owners of two great little theaters, NCT of San Diego and Manhattan. Gary and I go way back and I trust him implicitly. Kim, an actress (not the wannabe kind but the working kind with movies and lots of TV under her belt) will be our accompanist again. She's good and has prepared opening pieces, style pieces, etc. We are using our original tour intro music again, which feels like we pick up where we left off. Oh, and Gary and Kim are partners and soon-to-be married.

Like last tour, they have booked two good young players to go with us. Dorian and Chris are something else. Very talented and VERY fun. Dorian is about to be a dad and Chris is on his first excursion overseas. I love having them along.

We have so much drive time planned that we decided to watch the entire *Lord of the Rings* trilogy on the bus. And we did. Against a backdrop of changing Western European countryside.

Seven days and five shows later...

Walking in Wurzburg, the river, the vineyards, the castles, churches, architecture, cobbled streets with vibrant walking people, electric trains, and we find a café on the second level. I get a shot of Cuervo to wake up a bit; this time it comes with a slice of lemon. Dinner is great. I sit by Sylvio and we slip into talking about guitars, Taylors and Martins, this time. I feel a wave of gift. We weren't scheduled, planned, or otherwise meant to be here. We just ended up here through an ambling brook of little choices and it seems we may have been very fortunate. We sit across from a clay-colored cathedral with gothic spires reminiscent of the Duomo in Milan, but with clean plaster areas integrated into the gothic designs. Directly across from us is a lit ornate yellow building that could almost be a Gaudi with four floors and every window open, another subtle clue about something. I feel my attentiveness, my powerful attendance, building.

We leave the café and walk across the platz. Sylvio, a great source, wants to go left, but I'm sure we go right. The group stands on the corner leaning towards going Sylvio's way. Sylvio himself though is in attendance, too, I guess because he feels me walk my direction a short way and waits.

I am in front of a lovely old pub when eight or so lovely German women in their 20s surround me giggling and smiling, speaking German to me and holding an odd assortment of things. They are so happy, I just look at their faces chattering away at me. They realize I don't speak German and decide which of them will try English. There is one girl with stickers on her shirt and shoulders; she is beaming and beautiful and she is somehow the focus of their joy. I glance over at my group some distance away and they are all staring at me slack-jawed like hungry fisherman who just saw me catch a sailfish in a teacup.

I'm told the girl is to be married tomorrow. I smile and say, "No! Please, don't," as I join the game. I think they are giving little airplane bottles of flavored vodka away for two Euro to raise money in some bridal ritual for the pretty girl. I look down at the sticker on her tummy, and it says, "Baby." My band arrives on the scene lead by Dorian as I reach out to the young mommy and explain we'll have to dance in the street first. So she falls into a waltz with me right there. Like a dream this beaming bride-to-be and mommy's face is right there in a rotating sea of happy and mildly astonished faces as we waltz some circles on the sidewalk. The girls chatter; I have certainly caught the game. They suggest I kiss her for a bridal donation of two Euro (nope) and instead she wants to waltz again and steps into gear right away. After a few circles I say, "And this time we dip, yes?" and we do, her slightly bulging belly showing and she drops her lovely blonde head back, showing her glowing first-time mommy face to the night light of this old cobbled street. I buy a little bottle and chip in my two Euro for the bride. Time to walk on. The entire scene was less than two minutes probably. Questions come flying out of my group as to how I got into that and waltzed. I don't know, but as I look up, I see that I have chosen the right road in more ways than one as out hotel is glowing in the distance, a direct hit. Now, what kind of dope would miss these moments? Not I.

Monday morning, August 15, 2005, magic happened.

Waking in Wurzburg is a gift. The bells through my window, the gothic spires and towers all through the town are ringing a Catholic holiday, echoing off of the big river and stone bridges and the castles, blowing over and through the hillside vineyards and parks that surround the town, nudging the memories of last night from the sidewalk cafes and pubs in this small and beautiful town. I roll over to see a little radio on my wall in the overcast morning light so I turn it on and play soft classical music that is a flute with the Shanghai quartet, then a calm German male voice says something that I'm now sure meant, "Les McGehee, you are here and so here is the rest of the moment you've been looking for but didn't know it, here, be this." It is just long enough to get my ears ready for Norah Jones to finish me off with "my heart is drenched in wine," she knows she'll die in ecstasy, out across the deep blue sea, but she'll be "a bag of bones rolling down the road alone." I get my story from it, the beauty, the painful beauty of life, and the sadness of not being with my one. I cry, rubbing my head. The glory and the pain and life is so full I cry for everyone who doesn't see their customized cup brim, even though it does. Two birds communicate from some towers with a few caws in call and response; they use short sentences so as not to change the moment. I can faintly hear the angled falls/locks in the river, faintly hear the electric streetcar starting somewhere in town. Maybe all the beauty-loving folks of this town on a religious holiday morning are praying at the same time and I am collateral damage, caught in the crossfire of their perfect forever? I don't know when I've meant it more, but if this is it, who could complain? I cry again, this time more briefly. I know the moment is passing, but it is passing with a loving hand on me that slips away as slowly as it possibly can, using a beatific smile to replace its touch and ease the transition to the next moments, whatever they are. It says I'm being left in good hands. I'm so full and grateful the tears ebb at my eyes. My eternal moment waking in Wurzburg is a gift indeed, a very mighty gift. It wins and I lose, like the luckiest kid in existence.

Being given a glimpse into the infinite beauty through a moment like this is to give up previous knowledge as pointless. Future thought is for ungrateful dopes when a moment comes down on you like this. I am the improvised life and as I accept that thought the damn bells start up again, laughing for me. My life is natural today. The moment is a perfect place, beginning and end.

Six days and five shows later...

I don't know where I am. I peek out the window. No clues. I give. Now comes the last portion of the disorienting process...I don't care. I'll be getting on the bus in a few hours and we'll be going somewhere and doing the show, checking in to a hotel, looking for Internet and dinner. Instead of remembering where you are, you remember the flow of daily events, texture, little wins and losses. Like I remember I got to the gym yesterday; I bought a new phone card, got awarded a commendation on stage that was a colorful and excessively glowing certificate they referred to as an Honor Scroll, I think, but had to eat gross food twice. I just don't remember where in Germany they were. For a few days now it has been an acceptable practice to refer to a current hotel as "home."

Oddly enough, I totally remember where we are going. Baumholder. Furthermore, I know WHEN we are going: 11am. I also know that it'll take a few hours to get there and that I can't get to the gym before we leave—checked all that out. There're tour priorities for you.

Next day...

I am in Baumholder, Germany. Last night we rocked an ex-Nazi ballroom. They let us tour the underground bunkers and tunnel system from WWII. The previous show a few days earlier had been the Jimmy Buffet band and the Dallas Cowboy Cheerleaders. Surreal. We are now 12 shows in on 18 total. We do six one-nighters and then get a travel day. Monday we play in Belgium and Tuesday in the Netherlands.

Two days later...

We are killing at the NATO base in Belgium. The audience is so hot at the end of the replay that we just stop there. The Lt. Colonel (Romero) had helped us with a game set-up, now he and most everyone else there lines up for autographs, having pulled posters down and such. The commander gives us a medal commendation and it is a very cool one, kind of bigger than usual. We love those things. So far this tour, we've gotten a plaque, a Scroll of Commendation for Excellence to each of us individually, and three medals. Blush.

Our hosts lead the bus to one of their houses (Andre and Gabi's) and we have a great home-cooked meal complete with our favorites, fresh salad and crisp vegetables! Andre sends us out to his nice big, bad porch and the ice chest, and I open it. I hear Belgian angels sing; my Dad gasps in heaven and drools; our breath pauses: it is full of new Belgian beers like Chimay, local Hefeweissens, ales, oh, my. I look back over my shoulder at Andre and he gets hit with a wave of appreciation. Our hosts gather the appropriate glasses for each type of beer we choose. Tall glasses for the Hefes, open top goblets for the Chimay, ceramic mugs for the ale. SWEET. They even had good wine for Kim. Every beer drinker at the table, about 10 of us, drinks local beer except for Gabi, the only German in the room. She loves Budweiser in the can. She tells the story of the Anheuser family and how Budweiser was stolen from Germany. I can barely understand her, but she is such a lovely host and she keeps bringing me Chimays every time my glass gets low. SUUUWEEEEEET Gabi! We get stories about Saudi Arabia, share all our favorite places in Italy, share complaints about Egypt, praise Sharm al Sheikh and the Red Sea, etc. Andre had been quarterback at Prairie View A&M in Texas. A great night all around.

My last show of the tour...

We had a great show in Garmisch tonight. We are in the Alps and they are beautiful. The town is very quaint and the resort we are lodged in is very nice. We met some bizarre characters and celebrated late. I'll be going home, but they have a couple of dates left without me.

It's 1:30am and I bid a sad goodbye to the team. I hug them all. I think I have communicated significant support and gratitude to the young guys, but I'm missing Gary a little in the moment. When we hug, we hit each other like great durable toys. He's the shit, no doubt. That's in spite of and, perhaps, partially because I don't entirely agree with him. He is a lion of the industry, though, and one of the few improv producers I happily work for and with.

I pack a little before catching a two-hour nap before departure. Wow. Another tour wrapping up. The events have yet to sort in my mind. The rocking shows in Sembach; Ansbach; Scweinfurt; Baumholder; Bamberg; Chievres, Belgium; and now Garmisch, just to mention a few. And then there's the time and excursions in Holland, Wurzburg, Nurenburg, and others. Wow. I think, what if my run ended, who could complain?

I'm back home when I get the call from the team. Amazing they got to a phone together. They tell me that they miss me and have been setting a chair on stage for me in honor of my place on the team. I love those corny dopes.

FIVE BASIC RULES FOR IMPROV SCENES

Compiled by Tyler Bryce

If you intend to perform improvisation, you'll like this short list. It was compiled by a kid I trained and eventually named to be my first artistic director, my good friend, Tyler Bryce. He's not a kid anymore; he's played all over the place. These rules pretty much apply at all levels of skill. – Yer pal, Les

Improvisation is a unique form of theater in which the actor/actress is at the same time playwright and performer. Because it is spontaneous in nature, most people assume that improv is accidental art. In truth, Improv Theater is very similar to improvisational jazz. To be consistently successful, imagination must be blended with structure, individual skills, and ensemble play. Any theater company engaged in this type of theater spends a great deal of time developing group skills and a vocabulary of improvisation.

The following rules are from a list originally developed by the infamous Comedy Workshop.

1. **Establish information early in a scene!** Who are you? Where are you? What are you doing there? What is your relationship with the other players? You can't build a scene without first laying the foundation.

2. **Listen to your fellow players!** Build on what they are creating. Remember to use *Yes and.* Never deny a creation. Sacrifice your own ideas for the good of the improvisation. Assume that everything your fellow players say is important and a direction for the scene.

3. **Concentrate.** Everything that is created during an improv scene must be sustained. Information that is created during a scene should be reused later. The door you create must stay in the same place (and reopen the same way). The glass

you drink from cannot a) Suddenly appear in your hand, b) Change size, or c) Float in mid air until you are ready to grab it again. Be responsible for everything you and your fellow players create, both in mime and verbally. Don't change occupations, ages, relationships, etc. Concentrate!

4. **Try to forward the scene by making the action choice.** Avoid verbal traps like going into a story or remaining seated in a chair. Make the "where" an important part of the scene. Whenever you are in trouble, go back to the "where."

5. **Always work at the top of your intelligence.** Challenge your fellow players by making assumptions about them. Be aware of subtext. Use the subtext to direct the scene toward each other. *Why you are doing something is more important than what you are doing.* Avoid characters who are one dimensional and clownish. Use all your knowledge and experience and you will find that you create scenes that say something. Never forget Point of View!

PLAYS WELL WITH OTHERS:
THE GAMES

Quick Reference Guide to the Games in this Book

Thi*his section contains a quick reference to the games discussed in this book, in the order in which they appear in the
book. Refer to the page on which a particular game is discussed
in detail to find additional information on the game including
issues, options, common mistakes, and many, fun variations.*

UN Desk

Page Number: 26
Number of Players: 2 at a time, more can rotate in

The scene for *UN Desk* is simple enough: a desk outside the
Great Hall at the UN. All the workshop participants are delegates. We all speak each other's languages. We respond in
whatever language we are approached with. Two chairs are
handy for this exercise. They both face forward but slightly
inward and a few feet apart. The chair on the left is Player One
and they are the catcher. Player Two chooses a fun style of
gibberish language and enters to converse briefly with Player
One. Player One listens, responds; there is give and take.
Players can practice listening and communication skills and
agreement and empowerment and reuse pieces of language
that get introduced into the conversation. The results are
amazingly communicative. We all know what they are talking
about if they stay intent on each other. I'm not sure it communicates into print but it is an amazing little machine of an
exercise.

Everybody go!

Page Number: 80
Number of Players: 3 or more, groups

We all stand in a circle. One participant steps forward and says, "Everybody go..." and then does something. The group all says, "Yes!" together and then we all do that same thing. Try to do it the way it was done by the originating player. Then right away a new player steps out with their idea and says, "Everybody go..." and the process repeats. Go quickly; all say yes for real, and if you get hurt you are doing it wrong.

World's Worst

Page Number: 99
Number of Players: 2 or more, groups

In *World's Worst*, a topic is taken from the audience. It might be a celebration or other event where people get together—a wedding, for example. All the players line up across the back of the stage. Players step forward when inspired, taking turns offering the worst thing that might be seen or heard at a wedding. It gets a laugh or it doesn't. The player steps back into line and another takes the center spot with a new idea on the same theme. When there is a pause in ideas the host changes the topic. The players try to keep the center spot hot and keep things moving.

Alternate clapping

Page Number: 101
Number of Players: 2 or more, in pairs

This is a good exercise to use to get physically warm and focused for play. Two people face each other and one claps, then the other claps, repeat. They go on clapping alternately. The goal is to get evenly spaced claps and speed it up until it sounds like applause. Over 15 seconds or so you can start and go faster and faster until it breaks. Try again and improve on it.

Trust walk

Page Number: 101
Number of Players: 2 or more, small groups

Here is a great exercise that builds mutual trust and confidence and a sense of taking care of your play partner. Player One closes their eyes tightly. If they find this uncomfortable or they open their eyes uncontrollably, then a blindfold is OK to use. Player Two leads them verbally on a walk. Player Two can explain, "Walk forward towards my voice. Stop. Take a small step to your left. Now forward again." Etc. Take the blinded partner on a walk and experience doorways, halls, different qualities of light and sound indoors and outdoors. After a few minutes, trade roles and walk back.

Things in...

Page Number: 102
Number of Players: 2 or more, can be done solo

Used as a warm-up, *Things in* is a game where one player asks another to name five things in a category. For instance, name five things in Einstein's sock drawer or name five things in Angelina Jolie's purse. The other player gets to use their imagination to answer. This comes in handy later in performance games because you are ready to go when you list items or contents. This can also be played with friends all at the same time, and, yes, Party Reader, it can even be another drinking game, if you must. Let's say there are five of us in the living room. One of us names the title, such as five things in Mother Teresa's backpack. Then each person in the room must name an item. When it is complete, all take a swig or a shot or slap themselves or whatever you think is fun, and then right back into the next round taking turns.

Zig Zag Zor

Page Number: 103
Number of Players: 4 to 10

This is the warm-up that I have used the longest. It works best with four to eight people, but it's flexible. It is known alternately as Zip Zap Zop, Zig Zag Zorg, Bud Wise Er, Z cubed, etc. Players stand in a small circle. Player One looks clearly at another player and says, "Zig!" The player who received the zig looks clearly at any player and says, "Zag!" The player who received the zag looks clearly at any player and says, "Zor!" When "Zor!" is said, the person saying it simultaneously claps. The player who receives the zor looks at any player and says, "Zig!" Etc. So, it will sound like "Zig! Zag! Zor! (clapping at same time) Zig! Zag! Zor (clapping at same time) Zig! Zag! Zor! faster and faster. The game continues as fast as the players can maintain it, until someone makes a mistake.

Gibberish conversations

Page Number: 104
Number of Players: 2 or more, small groups

Always fun, the skills this game develops will help with a lot of different things, too many to explain at this stage of the process. To start with, just have fun with it and see if you can let it flow. It is an important exercise and has lots of performance and training applications as well.

Pick a style of gibberish. You can choose a style of gibberish either by paralleling a real language that you don't know and drawing from all the best-related references you can think of. Or you can choose a batch of sounds, a character choice, a sing-song tone; it's wide open. You and your partner attempt to speak the same language, devising it jointly by listening to each other well enough to use and reuse words that each other has used in the conversation. That lets it build specificity and credibility and get more interesting. It also is a challenge to find the strengths and weaknesses of your particular gibberish menu. It builds on how well the listener listens and the reaction time that allows the things said to be heard as important things. The more real the reactions, the more succinct the vocabulary, the better the conversations.

What are you doing?

Page Number: 105
Number of Players: 3 or more

What a great gamey game, mainly identified with the ComedySportz show. It is an excellent game amongst friends. Two players stand. Player One starts doing something active through mime, like pretending they are riding a bike. Player Two asks the question, "What are you doing?" The question isn't asked coyly or with character; it is fired at the player punctually. Player One must then answer with something active that has nothing at all to do with the activity they are doing. They might say, "Walking the dog." Then Player Two starts miming that activity, walking the dog. Then it's Player One's turn to fire the question, "What are you doing?" Player Two answers with something that has nothing to do with walking the dog. Perhaps they say, "Brushing the president's teeth." Immediately, Player One begins miming brushing the president's teeth.

This goes on as fast and as creatively as the players can go until one of them is eliminated for repeating something that was already said in the game, or hesitating, or saying something that in any way resembles what they were actively miming. When a player makes one of these mistakes they are eliminated and a different player gets a chance.

First Letter Last Letter

Page Number: 108
Number of Players: 2 or more, in pairs

Players stand or sit in pairs. Player One starts a conversation about anything they wish, for instance, "I sure like watching NBA games." Player Two responds to the conversation, but starts with a word that begins with the last letter used by Player One. In this case, Player Two might say, "Sure. Me, too." Now Player One will respond with a word starting with the letter O. Maybe, "Other sports stop too much, but basketball is quicker." This goes back and forth for a couple of minutes.

Ball Toss

Page Number: 109
Number of Players: 2 or more, groups up to 20

Take a tennis ball, a small, inflated ball, and a beach ball and pass them back and forth in a big circle of 10-20 people. You can pass by tossing the ball across the circle anywhere. Emphasize safety and soft throws. Emphasize that some balls will get dropped and that's no big deal.

Expert Definitions

Page Number: 112
Number of Players: 2 or more in pairs, small groups

Player One gives the other a gibberish word. Player Two then confidently gives the definition to that new word, citing its roots or origin or whatever else shows their expert knowledge on the subject. Every answer is correct. Then Player Two gets to offer a word to Player One for definition. It can also be done taking turns in small groups.

Two Eyes on Paper

Page Number: 113
Number of Players: 2 or more, in pairs

I've provided a worksheet on the next page so you can try this exercise, but you'll see that you can create your own full-size pages easily. Basically there is a blank sheet with two dots where eyes might be if you were drawing a face to fill the page.

I usually pass around a box of crayons and let everyone choose one each. Players form pairs and sit together. They'll need a flat surface to make it easy to draw on the *Two Eyes* sheet.

Be silent for the duration of the exercise. Player One makes a single mark on the page, perhaps an eyebrow over an eye. Player Two then adds a mark. Taking turns, they draw a face. This continues until there is a significant pause whereupon the players should consider if the drawing is finished. Once finished, Player One puts a letter at the bottom of the page. The next player adds a letter and they take turns until a name is formed. The name might be gibberish or a traditional title. Then players should share and comment on how it felt to lead or follow, the concepts of variable leadership, how neither is responsible but both are, etc. Sometimes you learn a lot on the second run. Be sure not to let the length of the exercise grow. It only takes a minute or so to do a picture once you settle into the process.

Yes and Party Planners

Page Number: 114
Number of Players: 2 or more in pairs, small groups

Two players face each other. Player One suggests they throw a party for their team. Player Two responds literally with, "Yes and," adding whatever he chooses. The players take turns *Yes anding* the other players suggestions and encouraging whatever direction and flow the thing takes. Let it develop to its most flagrant degree without forgetting the initial reason for the party. The plan may begin as an employee appreciation day and end as a concert in Hawaii; there are no limits, but it must build through *Yes and* responses. It's important to enjoy the other player's ideas. This exercise usually takes less than a minute.

Dance Diamond

Page Number: 114
Number of Players: 4 or more, and multiple groups of 4

You have four people stand in an open area. They stand about six or eight feet apart, as if at the points of a diamond. They all face the same direction, so three of them can see the one at the front clearly. The one at the front is called the Point Player. Music is played. I choose music that makes people move, but doesn't cause them to think too much. I've been known to use Motown (just about anything by the Funk Brothers), James Brown, Ray Charles, and the Beatles. Anyway, the Point Player is directed to create some movements, dance if they want to (everyone dances, but some like to pretend they are just moving about). The three players seeing the Point Player from behind must copy the movement in unison with the Point Player. When the Point Player turns 90 degrees, a new Point Player is created and they seamlessly continue with the new Point Player choosing their own movements. The three behind them now match the new movements. This continues.

Slogans

Page Number: 115
Number of Players: 2 or more, small groups

Slogans is played with two to 20 people. The game starts with a real product, say milk, or a specific brand of something like Krispy Kreme or Tide. Then the group starts throwing out ideas for the slogans that were *rejected* for the product. Exercise your creativity. There might be one idea offered or five, but as soon as there's a significant pause, take another product real fast and keep the tempo up.

Wrong Name

Page Number: 116
Number of Players: individuals or groups

In *Wrong Name*, a team or an individual takes a minute to choose things around the room, point at them, and firmly call them something that they in no way are. For instance, you might point at a chair and firmly call it, "Pudding!" But what if you called that chair, "Dog?" Perhaps you know that you called it a dog because you were thinking of its four legs. That would not be doing the exercise because it uses logic. The goal of this exercise is to shake you out of logic's death grip.

Things in Common

Page Number: 116
Number of Players: 4 or more, small to large groups

At a gathering have people talk in pairs for two minutes, then in different pairs for two minutes. Direct them to find interesting things in common. Uninteresting things would include, "We work at the same place. We both like movies." Mundane stuff like that doesn't help. But, "We were both cheerleaders in the eighth grade. We both love the movie *Casablanca*. We both bass fish competitively. We both traveled in remote Asia when we were 20 years old." These things change the way you see each other and create reinforcements in the fiber of your community.

One Touch

Page Number: 125
Number of Players: 2 to 20

One Touch can be played with some sheets of newspaper wadded up and wrapped in clear tape. That makes it kind of a ball about 8 to 10 inches in diameter. A beach ball is OK, but too slow. A roll of socks makes a pretty good ball, too. The goal is to keep the ball in the air and in play without anyone catching it and without the same player touching it twice in a row. In a circle, a player tosses the ball up. Another player gets to hit it one time, like with her open hand, usually, and then another player hits it. It's like tapping it into the air. There's no predictable sequence; players just operate instinctively getting out of the way, covering for each other, whatever it takes. See how long you can keep it up..

Kitty Wants a Corner

Page Number: 126
Number of Players: 10 or more, small to medium groups

This is a great kid's game. It is one of my favorite games to start a practice session with. It's especially good in groups of 10 or more. Players stand in a circle. One player is in the center. That player is "It." *It* walks up to a player in the circle and says, "Kitty wants a corner." The player in the circle replies with, 'Go ask my neighbor" and *It* walks to someone else and makes the same statement, "Kitty wants a corner." This continues. While this is happening other players try to make eye contact and sprint to trade positions before *It* can jump into one of their vacated spaces in the circle. While players dart back and forth trading places, eventually *It* gets into one of their vacated spots and now the new stranded player is "It" and play rapidly continues.

10 Characters

Page Number: 126
Number of Players: individuals or groups (taking turns)

One player takes the stage and goes into a character. When the character is established a bit, in say three to eight seconds, the director can yell, "Switch!" and the player on stage goes into a different character. This goes on for 10 characters in a row. Fellow players should support the character changes with appropriate responses. *10 Characters* should take a minute or a minute and a half at the most.

Counting Together

Page Number: 127
Number of Players: 4 or more, small groups

Counting can be done more than one way, but start like this. The group sits in a circle quietly. Someone says, "One." Someone says, "Two." The goal is to count comfortably up to

20 or more without any two players speaking at the same time. No patterns. Just whatever it is, it is, and did the group find its balance and ability to count up past 20? If it takes a few tries, which it often does, try counting down from 20 instead—it sometimes freshens the exercise.

Shakespeare and other Style Games

Page Number: 127
Number of Players: 2 to 6

Take a real event, like a friend's bad experience at a mall, and act it out in a style. Start with Shakespeare, but when you get the hang of it, try other combinations. You could try Little Red Riding Hood done in the style of the TV show "24." You could do the Dr. Phil Opera. You could do folk music about computer repair. Style and subject matter combinations have a lot of possibilities.

And a couple of extra games...

Hitchhiker

Number of Players: 4 at a time, more can rotate in

Four players play at a time. Get four ideas from the audience about who and how to be and one unusual destination. For example, you might get an Elvis impersonator, a pregnant rich lady, a preacher, and an angry man going to Las Vegas. Start with one player on the field in a mime car. They should begin the scene showcasing their character. They go on a drive and pick up their fellow players. As other players enter the car, everyone should transfer into their new character.

Object Freeze

Number of Players: 3 or more, small to medium groups

Three to ten players can play at a time. Gather some interesting and large objects and put them in a bag ahead of time. Keep them secret from the other players. Have the players take turns taking an object from the bag. They must improvise a use for the object other than its actual use (the object becomes a prop). Play with the prop until everyone gets their ideas out, then quickly switch to a new surprise object. Some groups call this game, Props.

IN THEIR OWN WORDS

*The Power of Improv and Play as told by Artistic
Directors and Veteran Players of Improv*

In my professionally improvised life, I have had approximately 250 resident players, nine artistic directors, and several stellar managers. I've had great fortune in finding great people. They put up with me, laughed with me, and translated my directives while keeping the companies exciting and successful. While we were together we had lives full of joy, surprise, and adventure. Here are some of their comments about improvising together.

— Yer pal, Les

Megan Flynn, master improviser, manager, director, producer, nurse

The most powerful thing I took away from my years of improvisational play is that when I found myself afraid to do something on stage (i.e., sing a song in an unfamiliar musical style), I realized that that was the time I needed to volunteer and **go first**. I found that facing my fear—getting it over with—removed the power from it. Whenever I went first, I could then relax and enjoy what followed. I could appreciate my fellow performers and their efforts—actively engage in the moment. When I waited and went last, I was so self-absorbed in my fear, I missed out on what was offered by my fellow players. By doing the thing I was most afraid of, I believe I became a stronger team player and I know I gained the confidence to take more risks as a performer and in life.

Tyler Bryce, veteran player, director, producer, founding member of many theaters

Very early in my improv career I was having a significant problem playing the opening game, "What Are You Doing?" When asked the question, "What are you doing?" I would freeze. My mouth would seize up and I would just stand there with a pained look on my face as I got called out once again. It was frustrating. I knew I could play the game. But when I actually played the game, I couldn't play the game.

You asked me if I had lots of ideas in my head when I was trying to answer the question. That was exactly what was going on. It was like I was staring at a menu of choices in my head and I was trying to find the right one. I was attempting to compare the merits of different ideas in my head. I was trying so hard to come up with funny ideas that I couldn't answer the question and play the game.

You told me that I should just commit to the first clear thought that entered my mind and let everything else go. You revolutionized the way I approached not only that game, but every game.

Instead of making myself responsible for the right answer, you taught me to trust that any of those answers were right if I'd commit to it with 100% energy and confidence. **In life, people are so busy trying to find the right answer that often they fail to act at the proper time.** Les, you taught me that the time is now and that the right thing to do is always there in front of me. Just start doing it and that will become obvious. Your brain will catch up...lead with a choice.

Donna Kay Yarborough, veteran improviser, actress, obscure referrer, inspiration

Here's a secret to dealing with cancer: you have to be present in the moment. You cannot dwell on when and how things started in the past, and you cannot dwell on a future that may or may not come. You have to deal with what you have at the current time, take each new element for what it is without prescribing it as a reprieve or a death sentence, and, most importantly, focus on and savor each waking moment without expectation of outcome. These are skills that everyone should innately have—it's part of being human. But, as with many other aspects of ourselves, our fast-flowing culture has flushed these skills out of our consciousness. Had I not spent time with Les and the ComedySportz folks, I would have never re-discovered how to live in the present moment, and I would not be alive today.

Christine Walters, veteran player, producer

A few years ago, at the University of Texas, I had the pleasure of working with Les at an MBA intensive that included a week long series of improv courses. The day we were all introduced to the MBA students, the department heads, one by one stood behind the podium, and in that scholarly monotone voice explained the purpose of the program. The students seemed bored and unsure of this method of using improv as tools to aid in teaching business and communication lessons. Their doubts dissipated the minute Les stepped on the platform to speak. Stepping away from the podium, he connected with the audience. He explained what our intent was, gave an example of the power of *Yes and*, demonstrated **the importance of play**, and had everyone laughing and wanting to learn more. His voice, body language, leadership, and humor energized and inspired everyone in that room, including myself. At the end of the week-long course, students continued to approach the improv teaching staff, expressing how helpful the experience had been and insisting that every MBA student should have to attend in the future. Les McGehee is one of those incredible people who is always teaching lessons in life and laughter.

Les combines learning and working while maintaining a fun environment. One day, as Les and I were leaving a conference, Les turned to a gentleman and asked about his day. The man furrowed his brow and with a very serious face and tone said, "Very good, we did something important today." When the gentleman asked about Les' day, Les said, "We had fun."

Frankie Benavides, veteran player, extraordinary multi-language improviser, kidney donor

One thing I've learned [from you] is that the spontaneity and ability to flow you cultivate while doing this art form will spill over into every other area of your life. **Great things come from just doing something**, anything, no matter what that something happens to be. Using improvisation as a metaphor for life, you get first hand experience of the fact that your choices don't matter as much to your success as your ability to commit to them and passionately live them out.

"Mad Dog" Murray Harvel, veteran player, producer, auditor

It was 20 years ago when Texas' newly installed state auditor held his first ever staff meeting with over 300 employees. I was a 25-year old programmer who had just been promoted to assistant state auditor sitting on the front row of the auditorium next to my boss. The state auditor's first question to this room full of auditors was, "What does it take to be a professional?" No one answered. So he asked again, "Come on now, what does it take to be a professional?"

Finally, I blurted out, **"It's an act; it's a performance!"** My boss began to slink down in his chair when the state auditor exclaimed, "Correct...to *be* a professional, you have to *act* like a professional. From now on, as member of this office, we are all going to *be* professionals." It was several years before I thought of this meeting again.

Still working as an assistant state auditor, I answered an open audition call for a new improvisational comedy troupe in Austin and was selected. Having never done improv before, I soaked up the training like a sponge for months when I had an epiphany...this improv training was helping me to better "perform" as an assistant state auditor and to "act" like a real professional, just as the state auditor had talked about over two years before. This "state auditor" persona I envisioned, and then performed, in my job was no different than the numerous personas I was given each week by the audience and then envisioned and performed on stage. Also, my ability to answer questions on the fly (i.e., "thinking on my feet") during contentious audit meetings became much easier due to my improv training and performances. Even the scary feeling that I had just before going into an audit client's office to ask questions about fraud or mismanagement was exactly the same as the stage fright I felt just before going on stage Saturday night to perform as "Mad Dog" Murray. I had even learned to contain and control these scary feelings. Improv ruled.

Kelly Hanson, veteran player, artistic director, producer

Les inspires us to **use improvisation to continually open our minds**. His insights to improv have raised my emotional IQ in life!

Rachel Madorsky, veteran player, producer

My ComedySportz experience was one of the best experiences of my life. One of the great things I learned from Les and the amazing ComedySportz Community was the phrase, **"Got Your Back."** I love that we'd say this to each other just before taking the stage. Saying these words set an intention. A reminder and a pledge to myself and everyone that we are here for each other, that no one is alone up there, and that every idea will be supported. It is a great way to start a show - or any team endeavor. I say this to everyone I perform with, every show. Thank you, Les!

Britain Spellings, veteran player, TV and film actor

I had been talking to you, asking for a raise for teachers. It made me really angry and I wanted to continue talking, but I had to go back to teaching...COMEDY. I was fuming mad and I had to snap back into funny guy mode. And I did. I went straight from your office to the stage and got under way. And I gave one hell of a class. I was on fire. I had a tremendous amount of confidence. I was, somehow, able to funnel all that anger into my performance. I think that was an invaluable skill that I learned in that moment and it has served me well on my long journey in the industry.

I finished the hour and put the class on break and walked right to the door and out to my car. I had to get out of there. I drove around for about 10 minutes. I was thinking of all the things I needed to say to you—things that would surely make you understand my position. When I came back you were in the parking lot waiting for me. I opened my door and we looked at each other. You were the first to speak. What you said was the most perfect thing you could have said. It was like I had said all the things I had been thinking and you were addressing those things. I instantly felt 97% better. All that anger just went away and we were back to where we started. I learned from that, too. **I learned how our community was just that—a community.** And I was happy to be a part of it. You just knew me so well after only a couple years and you knew what to say.

By the way, I think you did give us that raise, so thanks for that. And for all the lessons I learned that have helped me in my professional and personal life. I am grateful I found you guys—ComedySportz, Les, Megan, Tyler, et al. That's where it all started for me.

Gary Kramer, veteran improviser, producer, improv mogul

Les is a singular talent, with an enormous passion for life. He is a man of tremendous homespun charm and wit, and **he is much smarter than a guy from Texas ought to be.** I have traveled across the globe with him—spent hundreds of hours on planes, buses, ferries, and jitneys; logged countless nights performing in theaters, clubs, tents and bars—and I still don't understand anything he talks about. It definitely sounds like he knows what he's saying, though, so I always pay close attention. Les is brilliant, talented, charming, and terribly clever. But I'm taller than he is, so I win.

IN THEIR OWN WORDS

The Power of Improv and Play as told by Business Clients

I have had the good fortune of finding some amazing, diverse professionals to enjoy my time with. I'm thrilled to be associated with them. In the moments when I share group mind with these people they look like they are glowing to me. Their influence and support has had a profound effect on my life and work.

I believe these associations are no accident. Like a good improvisation, it is how it should have gone. Moments conspired to quietly lead us to each other. These people blur the lines between spiritual friend, business associate, and client. I have taught and learned many things with these people. I feel like they have unique perspectives and insight into what I do.

These are comments from some of those people...

Steven Tomlinson, Ph.D., professor, award-winning playwright

An afternoon working and playing with Les McGehee will increase your powers of observation and your spontaneous creativity—and you learn how to really *listen* to others. His workshops leave my students feeling smart, energized, and more powerfully connected to each other.

After working with Les, I adopted **"Yes, and..." as a spiritual discipline**, and it's gradually becoming a reflex to see obstacles as opportunities in disguise. The practice has proven a reliable source of inspiration for writing, teaching, and harmony in relationships. These days, my best ideas for plays come from the creative tension of yes/and.

Sharon Sutton, educator, administrator, performer

I have so valued my improv training and experience. The *Yes and* is a wonderful tool to communicate with both at home and work. I have brought this into the leadership programs that I develop and feel that everyone who hears it and practices comes away a better listener and team member. Really listening to each other and making sure that you are both connected are also great life tools.

The best part about improv is that it is all about each other and not one person shining on their own.

Priscilla Hicks, award-winning event planner, inspiration, collaborator

One of my favorite stories about working with you is the wonderful save you made for us. We were at the Granite Shoals trip and we had ordered a treasure chest that was supposed to come with 50 keys—one of which would open the box. **We thought we had it planned perfectly, but wouldn't you know,** it turned out that more than one key worked. The first lady to try opened it—much to my shock. Your fast thinking saved the day when you jumped on the chest and stopped her from opening it—all in character of course. Your improv proved invaluable and gave us days of mileage out of that treasure chest!

Thanks for being the professional that came to our rescue!

Chris Bacorn, Ph.D., MPA, CHE, educator, administrator

When I first met Les McGehee I was skeptical, **"Games at work? C'mon.** Maybe at the Christmas Party. Hey, healthcare is serious business, sometimes life or death." That was four years ago. Since then Les has won me over completely. His lighthearted, humorous approach to having fun at work is just what we need, especially in healthcare. What's more, Les' games carry a subtle, important message: "This work is just too important to take seriously." Les has made me a believer.

Leslie Jarmon, Ph.D., professor, administrator, social guru

What can I say but "glorious"?

As a specialist in professional and academic communication, I have witnessed repeatedly the immediate success of McGehee's improvisation methods in transforming individuals and groups into people who are creative, open, imaginative, and respectful risk-takers. **People undergo a profound change in outlook**—and have fun doing it.

Gail Bentley, Ph.D., RN, educator, administrator

Les "levels the playing field" by introducing games, activities that make everyone stop and think about how they communicate. We are now incorporating the experiential activities into our supervisory classes. The employees have fun and it just so happens they are also learning how to communicate more effectively.

Our supervisors still talk about how they use some of the activities that Les taught them in their staff meetings...**especially when staff seem to be at an impasse or are unwilling to see different options for solving problems.** The non-threatening nature of the exercises puts staff at ease and facilitates participation by all. Requests for Team Building training has greatly increased as word got out that the training was fun, practical, and worked.

David Perkoff, producer, musician, event planner, writer

At work and in our associations, we can do all the assigned tasks and never really be passionate, never really care; we're just showing up to that career track and running the paycheck race. I don't believe that's really being involved. In music and the arts, it's not great until every cell, every emotion, every fiber of your being is engaged in the project at hand. When you go all the way and release your inner 'chi' to your craft, that's when you really get some action and if you have the skills to go with reaching deep, then you can really, really influence others.

Everyone has been to a concert where the players were play-ing skillfully, singing the songs, accurately performing the music but the energy just wasn't there. And I'm sure you read-ers have all been to at least one event that was so moving and powerful that you wanted to cry or laugh or both at the same time. Well, those occasions happen when the performer has gone all the way inside themselves and mucked about in the primal flow. With practice, they can get really good at sculpt-ing that energy and sharing it.

Being involved isn't just about making some calls and some emails and building consensus. Being involved is about get-ting all of your personal energies lined up and ready.

Owen Eggerton, veteran player, artistic director, author, fan of Les

I, Owen Eggerton, learned everything good I know from Les. I was worthless before I met Les and I tend to lean towards worthlessness when I'm away from him for too long. When I have to go on stage without Les I sometimes pee like a shivering, scared little teacup poodle. I've gotten used to it. I do it in private now. If I know I have to perform without Les I often wear one of the shirts I borrow from him (but don't return) and I wear it in front of a mirror talking in Texas twang and squinting my eyes enough to fool myself that he is there with me. Then, I usually pee like a teacup poodle anyway. This has greatly irritated the ugly rash I have all over my lower body.

Les introduced me to my wife. I could kill him. I'd be getting so many hot chicks right now instead of babysitting my toddler. But how can you hold onto anger against such a good guy? Besides, my wife is better than I deserve. Please, don't print that, Les, because I don't want her to realize how true it is. She might leave me for a man with a real job.

In the future I hope we are all more Les-like. Or at least that I am. Les should be president. And not just of America. And he smells nice. **I wrote this, not Les.**

–Yer pal, Owen

ABOUT THE AUTHOR

Les is a working comedian and improvisation pioneer who has entertained and trained millions of happier people throughout the U.S. and the world. He has toured through 11 countries and performed thousands of shows.

Les and the National Comedy Theatre have been featured on ABC, WB, Fox Family, and PBS. His writing credits include a book and many successful scripts and published articles. He has played with famous, and not-so-famous, stars of stage and screen including appearances with cast members of *Saturday Night Live*, *Whose Line is it Anyway?*, *MadTV*, *The Simpsons*, and others.

After years of successful improv comedy performances, Les began answering requests to teach improvisation to diverse groups and businesses. Whether teambuilding for AT&T, providing leadership training for the Department of Veterans Affairs, or riffing on business skills training for prestigious graduate schools of business, Les gets rave reviews.

His many accomplishments include being a founder of ComedySportz, National Comedy Theatre, IMPROVMBA, and other companies; a three-time winner of the World Series of Comedy in Kansas City; a featured performer at The Comedy Store in Los Angeles, and at the HBO Showcase; the Comedy League of America's National Improv Champion, 2001-2002; and the National Comedy Theatre's "Tour for the Troops" in 2004 and 2005.

Les lives in Austin, Texas with his wife Christina and their daughters Marina and Lucia. Family, friends, music, and laughter keep Les very happy.

Contact Les!

Questions, inquiries, or comments for Les can be sent via email to *les@lesmcgehee.com*.